Dedication

For my wife, Irene, you make me so very happy. You are my forever love, my partner, my peace, my greatest adventure.

Table of Contents

The Swiss Lake Syndicate Murders

Robert Colling

Published by: Book Publish Pro

Chapter One

Detonation

"Hello, it's wonderful to meet you, Mr. Iglesia. My name is Mr. Lutz, and I am the director of this lab. I'll be taking you on a full tour momentarily."

The man's voice quivered slightly, and he paused to wipe a slick sheen of sweat from his brow with a handkerchief that was too damp to be useful. His white lab coat, meant to inspire trust, looked slightly wrinkled and hastily buttoned. His glasses, round and thick, kept slipping down his nose. "Is this your first time visiting Switzerland?"

At first, Mr. Iglesia said nothing. He simply looked Lutz up and down, cataloguing him like he would a new shipment—clinical, unhurried, and wholly unimpressed. Lutz was precisely the sort of man who rose through bureaucratic institutions not by talent but by attrition. The last man standing. No doubt, he had survived enough funding cuts and failed projects to eventually inherit the title of *director* simply because there was no one else left.

Iglesia adjusted his charcoal grey overcoat and then took it off and hung it on a nearby hook. He offered a tight, polite smile, though there was no warmth behind it. "Look, I'd like to make the most of our time together," he said, "You know who I am and who I work with. It's a syndicate. There, I said it. And let me add," he took a step closer, "not all syndicates are bad. We always seem to have lots of money, and we're generously funding your efforts here. I've told the other regional directors that I'm on the verge of announcing a new revenue stream. One that would supposedly double the syndicate's global profits within a year." His voice was calm, clipped, and efficient. "Why don't you show me why you set up this little 'meet and greet'?"

Lutz froze, then chuckled nervously, unsure if he should laugh or apologize. He settled on both, producing a jittery sound that landed somewhere between a hiccup and a whimper.

Iglesia let the moment hang for effect, then continued. "I believe I was scheduled to be here at exactly 16:30. I'm hoping that a quick tour will take no more than thirty minutes. After that, you can take me to your favorite local restaurant for some fondue and profit projections. And maybe jot down a list of worthwhile places to see while I'm in Switzerland."

Lutz straightened, clearly relieved to be given clear instructions. "That sounds like a great plan. Please, sir, follow me."

They moved through a long, sterile corridor lined with recessed LED lighting. A faint hum echoed along the corridor—machines, ventilation systems, or maybe just the building sighing from age and pressure.

They stopped at an oversized, matte-metal security door with no visible handle. Lutz leaned in and aligned his eye with a small glass circle on the wall. A quiet *click* confirmed his retina had passed inspection. The lock turned green.

"This way," Lutz said, stepping aside to allow Iglesia in first.

What lay beyond exceeded Iglesia's already-high expectations. The lab sprawled in all directions, a sleek maze of immaculate white surfaces, chrome instruments, and floor-to-ceiling glass partitions. Clean rooms buzzed with activity. Technicians in everything from standard lab coats to full hazmat suits moved with focused urgency within their spaces.

Rows of centrifuges spun quietly. Beakers bubbled. Robotic arms shifted back and forth with meticulous precision, tending to samples with the care of a jeweler polishing rare gems. The scent of isopropyl alcohol and ozone lingered in the air—pure sterility.

Lutz began narrating as they walked, as though trying to prove his usefulness. "Each of these labs focuses on a separate step in our gene research protocols. The safety and decontamination standards exceed WHO regulations. Every item brought in or out is tracked, sanitized, and logged into our master server."

Iglesia nodded, walking just behind and to the side of the director. Besides the tour information, he was, and by his nature, studying every door they passed. He made mental notes of emergency exits, the location of fire extinguishers, even the weight of the glass panes—thicker than usual.

They arrived at the final room at the far end of the hallway. Glass-walled, clean, humming with power. Along the back wall rose three towering racks of servers, blinking with sequences of red, green, and white LED lights.

Lutz paused, standing proudly at the entrance like a man about to reveal a prized secret. "This is the heart of our operation."

Iglesia raised an eyebrow. "Impress me. The syndicate didn't spend a fortune on white walls and blinking lights. What's the return on our investment?"

Lutz beamed, gesturing through the glass. "That piece of equipment in the center—do you see it? That is a one-of-a-kind, state-of-the-art gene splicer and sequencer. It connects to every other server here. Years of algorithmic refinement, protein folding simulations, machine learning—all leading up to what it can now do."

Iglesia squinted at the machine. It didn't look like much—roughly the size of a copier with tubes feeding into the sides and a narrow metallic strip across the front.

"And what exactly *can* it do?" Iglesia asked, crossing his arms.

"We've nearly perfected a gene patch that regrows human hair."

Iglesia's expression didn't change, but his silence spoke volumes.

Lutz rushed to clarify. "No, no, no. I know what you're thinking." He held up both hands as if to slow Iglesia's reaction. "But the global hair-loss industry is a nearly four-billion-dollar annual market. Just imagine! No more pills, no more transplants. This is a gene patch—simple, efficient. We insert it, and in a few days, dormant follicles are reactivated."

"Hair gene patches," Iglesia repeated flatly. "That's why I'm here?"

Mr. Lutz continued unabated. "Any age, gender, ethnicity—it works for all. We're finalizing human trials now. The cost? Ten to thirty thousand dollars per client, and it'll fly off the shelves. But here's the key: we're not looking to build retail clinics. That's not our model."

Iglesia turned toward the exit. "You're right. That's not *our* model. Goodbye."

He made three steps toward the fire door exit before Lutz lunged forward and blocked his path. "Wait! Please—just wait a second!"

Iglesia glared but allowed him to speak.

"You don't understand!" Mr. Lutz caught Iglesia's glare. "I mean, I'm not telling it right. The syndicate won't have to *own* any clinics or stores. Every patch will be licensed. Every clinic that wants to use it will have to pay *you*. That's where the big money is. Not the product—*the patent*! The exclusive rights. Imagine global control over technology that every cosmetic clinic in the world *needs.*"

Iglesia paused, just for a moment, as if reconsidering.

That's when the blast hit.

A shockwave tore through the facility. Walls buckled. Alarms shrieked. A fireball, furious and sudden, erupted and flew down the hallway with a deafening roar. The windows to the server room shattered outward. One of the ceiling panels tore loose and killed a nearby technician.

Lutz was thrown into Iglesia, and both men went sideways.

The few sprinklers that were left hissed to life, spraying from the ceiling in rhythmic pulses. Red lights flashed. A computer voice repeated over the PA system in German and English:

"Emergency protocol activated. Please evacuate immediately. This is not a drill."

Smoke billowed from a ruptured gas line near the centrifuge stations. A second explosion—smaller, but closer—rattled the lights above.

Outside, sirens could be heard approaching—fire, ambulances, possibly police. Many boots ran upstairs to find blast damage, blood, and human remains.

Chapter Two

Swissair

Dylan woke slowly from her brief attempt at sleep. She could never manage the recommended hours of rest on any long-haul flight, and this seven-hour Swissair trip to Zurich was no exception. Though the cabin lights were dimmed and the rhythmic hum of the engines should have lulled her to sleep, the new case kept working its way back into her thoughts, disrupting any chance of relaxation.

She blinked slowly, rubbed her temple, and glanced around the dimly lit first-class cabin.

"Can't sleep?" came a familiar voice beside her. Dillon was stretched out in the first-class bed adjacent to hers, eyes half-closed, but aware.

Dylan lowered the partition between them and whispered, “You sleep. I’ll find a movie, or I’ll run through this dossier that Mr. Haus gave us again.”

Dillon gave a sleepy nod. Within moments, soft snoring began to rise from his side of the partition. She smiled faintly and let the wall slide back up before turning her attention to the screen in front of her.

She scrolled through the in-flight movie selection, half-heartedly reading titles and thumbnails. Nothing caught her interest—at least, nothing she hadn’t seen or ignored before. With a sigh, she reached into her carry-on and her hand hit first on the latest novel by Samatha Blaese.

The Starry Night Train Mystery Murder.

The cover was typical Blaese—bold red letters, a shadowy train disappearing into the desert, and two unmistakable silhouettes in trench coats, clearly modeled after herself and Dillon. Dylan flipped the book over to read the synopsis.

"A train, a murder, and some very rich people...this is how the second installment starts, and the mystery only grows from there. Reconnect with our two detectives as they follow the clues and look for evidence to solve a wealthy man's murder. And, instead of battling crime, they will have to battle the feelings they have for one another."

She snorted. It was half a laugh and half a groan, loud enough to earn a few hushed "shhh"s from passengers nearby. Dylan ducked down in her seat, smiling sheepishly.

Sure, she and Dillon had formed a business partnership. Yes, they had talked about what that commitment meant. And yes, she'd opened up to him in ways she never had with anyone else—especially after her father's death. But leave it to Samatha Blaese to twist everything into a slow-burning romance plot wrapped in a mystery. The mystery might be the excuse for the story, but the way Blaese wrote it, their "will-they-won't-they" was the real hook.

And the worst part?

Dylan wasn't entirely sure the author was wrong.

She opened the paperback, and a 3x5 index card slipped out, landing softly in her lap. She picked it up and read, eyes widening as she scanned the note.

"Hello, my lovelies, I hope this latest case proves as juicy as your last one. A special thanks to Dillon for sending me a synopsis of your last case. By the way, I changed the ending to make one of the rich kids the

killer. Artistic license, and it reads better that way. Kisses and bye for now!"

Dylan stared at the card for a long second, then lowered the partition again and nudged Dillon hard in the shoulder.

He startled upright, blinking. "What? I'm up! What's going on?"

She thrust the card into his lap.

"Samantha Blaese is what's going on. It says here you've been in touch with her. She thanks you for sending her a *synopsis* of our last case. Care to explain?"

Dillon rubbed his face and yawned. "She texted. Asked how we were. Wanted a few case details. I sent her a short reply. That's all."

"Why would you answer her text?" Dylan hissed.

"I thought it might be good PR. She's got a fanbase, and who knows, she might even refer new clients someday. It was innocent, I swear." Dillon slid back down beneath his blanket, clearly hoping the topic would die a natural death. "Don't be mad, okay?"

Dylan let out a frustrated breath and slid the partition up again without answering. She picked up the book and tried to read, but her thoughts wouldn't let her. Were they... *in a relationship*? More than business partners? She cared about him. That much was obvious. But what they had was best described as complicated. It always had been right from the start.

By the time the cabin lights brightened for breakfast service, she had read only five pages. Her mind kept going back to Sam's card.

****

As the plane began its descent into Zurich, many opened their window shades to reveal the early morning light breaking across the jagged horizon. Sunlight crept through the clouds and poured over snow-dusted peaks, painting the Swiss landscape in a glorious, golden hue.

Dylan stared out the window, momentarily breathless. The lakes shimmered blue-green in the valleys below, flanked by neat patches of farmland and the occasional scatter of brown-roofed chalets. She wasn't usually one for scenic awe, but even she had to admit—this was something else.

Dillon lowered the partition again, clutching a cup of coffee. "Beautiful, isn't it? And these aren't even the Alps yet."

She nodded. "I'm officially impressed."

They touched down smoothly, and after clearing customs and grabbing their luggage, they spotted a man holding a sign that read, *DYLAN AND DILLON*. Next to him stood another man, sharply dressed in an expensive black coat.

"Mr. Haus, I presume?" Dylan extended his hand.

Mr. Haus ignored it. "Follow me. The driver will take you to your hotel."

And that was that. No pleasantries, no small talk.

They followed him to a sleek black sedan. The trunk popped open, and the driver loaded their bags with robotic efficiency. The ride into Zurich was silent; the only sounds were the quiet hum of the car and the occasional GPS instruction in German. Mr. Haus sat upright and unsmiling in the front passenger seat.

Once they arrived at the hotel, a charming yet modern building tucked into a quiet part of the new city. Haus turned slightly in his seat.

“I will return at 8:00 a.m. sharp tomorrow to escort you to the lab. Be prepared.” Without another word, he stepped out of the car and disappeared into the city.

The driver opened the trunk, deposited their bags on the curb, and gave a slight nod before returning to the vehicle and driving off.

Dillon shook his head. “He wasn’t much of a conversationalist.”

“There was a distinct chill in the air,” Dylan agreed, hoisting her bag over her shoulder. “Let’s get checked in.”

Their hotel suite had two bedrooms and a shared sitting area, with a panoramic view of Lake Zurich stretching outside the windows. Dylan dropped her bag on the couch and walked over to the window. The water was perfectly still, reflecting the soft colors of the morning sky like a giant mirror. She could just make out the outline of the mountains on the horizon.

Dillon came in behind her. “Not bad for a work trip.”

“Feels a bit surreal,” Dylan admitted. “Almost too peaceful.”

He nodded, then pulled out his phone. “Want to grab a coffee downstairs? Or a walk down to the lake? Might be the only downtime we get.”

She glanced at him. “Coffee and a walk sound good.” Then she paused. “But no Blaese talk, okay?”

“Deal,” he said, holding up his hands.

They strolled through the hotel’s café and took their lattes to a table near the window. Dylan finally allowed herself to breathe. Despite the jetlag and the awkward plane conversation, something about being here settled her. Maybe it was the distance from everything familiar. Or maybe it was the anticipation of the case. Whatever it was, she felt focused.

“We should review what we know,” she said.

Dillon nodded. “Right. Mr. Iglesia was killed in a lab explosion somewhere near Zurich. He was the Syndicate’s man, and from what we’ve heard, they think it wasn’t an accident.”

“And we’ve been hired to find out who killed him, why, and whether it was someone inside the lab—or someone trying to send a message to the Syndicate,” Dylan added. “Which is, in every way, terrifying.”

Dillon took a slow sip of his drink. “You worried?”

“I’m always worried when billion-dollar criminals call us by name.”

“Fair enough.”

They sat in silence for a while, watching sailboats drift lazily across the lake. The peace wouldn’t last. It never did. But for now, in this quiet corner of Switzerland, it was enough.

Dylan glanced sideways at Dillon. “Tomorrow’s going to be intense.”

“Yeah,” he said. “But we’ve been through worse.”

“I suppose we have.”

He leaned back in his chair, arms behind his head, and said teasingly, “Think Blaese will turn this one into a book, too?”

Dylan smiled despite herself. “Only if we survive it.”

Chapter Three

The Syndicate

The next morning, Dylan and Dillon stepped out of the hotel's breakfast restaurant into the marble-tiled lobby. The air smelled faintly of roasted coffee beans and polished wood. Seated guests murmured over their croissants and newspapers while a pianist played something slow and jazzy in the corner. It was almost enough to make Dylan forget they were on a case.

Almost.

Standing near the revolving doors, pacing slowly with his hands clasped behind his back, was Mr. Haus. His posture was perfect, spine straight as a sword, and his expression remained the same unreadable blend of sternness and calculation.

“I hope you slept well,” he said, his voice neutral, eyes sweeping over them without warmth.

Dylan raised an eyebrow but said nothing. She doubted he hoped for anything of that kind. She followed him out to the curb, where a sleek black SUV waited. Dillon slid in first, Dylan followed, and Mr. Haus took the front passenger seat. The driver, a stone-faced man in mirrored sunglasses, shifted into gear without a word.

“Where's the lab?” Dillon asked as they merged into Zurich's morning traffic.

“We'll be taking a short drive along Lake Zurich to a small town called Männedorf,” Haus said. “The lab is located on a hill above the town. Originally, the building was a convent. In the 1960s, it was taken over by a large group of hippies—spiritual seekers, dropouts, social outcasts. They squatted there for years until the building fell into disrepair and foreclosure. The Syndicate acquired the land in the eighties and rebuilt it as a state-of-the-art laboratory. Chem research, pharmacology, and some biotech."

Dylan glanced at Dillon, who was watching the lake roll by through the window. Then she turned her attention to Haus.

"Why don't you like us?" she asked bluntly.

The car was quiet for a beat too long. Then Haus replied without turning. "Thank you for being direct with me. Allow me to be equally direct. I was against hiring you both. From the beginning."

He paused to adjust his coat and continued. "I currently serve as legal counsel to the Syndicate. When the matter of investigation came up following the bombing, I recommended three other detective firms—firms with long-standing reputations and far more experience. I was overruled."

Dylan crossed her arms. "We may not have a hundred cases under our belts, but—"

"You've solved two," Haus interrupted. "Two high-profile cases, yes. But two."

"What I was going to say, if you'll let me finish," Dylan said icily, "is that we have years of experience—individually—working for other agencies before we partnered. Those cases were classified. Off the record. Doesn't mean they didn't happen."

Haus's tone remained clinical. "Perhaps. But the only reason you're here is because you owed Mr. Iglesia a personal favor. The Syndicate believed that debt would motivate you to do a thorough job."

Dillon finally turned from the window. "The dossier you left us mentioned that Iglesia had a widow. Curious."

"Is it?" Haus replied, voice unreadable. "Then I suppose now is a good time to introduce you to the Syndicate's structure."

He turned slightly, just enough for Dylan to catch the hard edge of his profile.

"There are five principal directors," he said. "Each one oversees an entire continent or major region. One for the Americas. Two for Asia—North and South. One for Africa. And the late Mr. Iglesia represented all of Europe. Now, his widow Vyra has assumed his position, at least temporarily."

Dillon frowned. "Will we be able to meet all of them in person? Or are we talking about secure Zoom calls and veiled threats?"

Haus allowed a thin, humorless smile. "You will meet each of them face-to-face. That's been arranged. I'll be present at every meeting."

"Of course you will," Dylan muttered.

Haus continued without acknowledging the comment. "Bringing all five directors to the same building is, to put it mildly, unprecedented. It's never happened before. They agreed to convene at the lab because each one suspects the other. And because none of them believe anyone would be foolish enough to plant another bomb with everyone in the same place."

"And they're not allowed to leave until the case is solved?" Dylan asked.

"That's correct. And you have one week."

Dylan blinked. "One week may not be long enough..."

"One week," Haus repeated. "No extensions. This was decided by vote, and I do not believe you will get another."

Dillon folded his hands. "So, we're essentially being forced into a process-of-elimination approach. If the facts point to one of them, fine. But if they don't..."

"Then you better be very convincing," Haus said flatly. "But let me share my thoughts, since I've been dealing with these individuals for over a decade. Each member of the Syndicate climbed the ranks not by force or intimidation—but by generating revenue. Money is what matters. Unlike what you see in crime movies, they don't eliminate each other to rise. The bombing disrupts that order. It suggests chaos. And the Syndicate hates chaos."

Haus grew more serious, leaning forward.

"I considered the possibility of a rival syndicate," he said. "But no other organization is big enough. Not even close. Nor would an underling act on their own—they wouldn't survive the day, which leaves us in an impossible bind. The widow? We checked. Rock-solid alibi. Zero financial motive. And she passed all internal diagnostics. She's either innocent or a master manipulator."

"We'll keep her in mind," Dillon said carefully.

"We're also reviewing all lab personnel," Haus added. "Emails, messages, activity logs. If there's a thread to pull, we'll find it."

Dylan took a breath. "Fine. We'll begin by interviewing the other directors. But I don't want you in the room."

Haus turned his head slowly. "Not possible. But don't worry. Everything will be recorded anyway. Cameras are everywhere. We'll be watching whether I'm present or not."

The SUV continued climbing as the narrow mountain road twisted higher. The lake below was now a distant blur of silver blue. The surrounding landscape transformed into forest—thick evergreens brushing against mist, as if trying to hide the old secrets embedded in the hillside.

Finally, they rounded a bend, and the lab came into view.

It was a large, rectangular, three-story building, clearly once a place of worship or quiet retreat. But the peaceful history was marred now. The entire left wing had collapsed, blackened, and crumbled. Police tape flapped in the wind, cordoning off the affected section. Two drones hovered nearby, buzzing like flies.

The car stopped at the front steps.

Dillon stepped out and took a long look down the mountain. "Spectacular view," he said, whistling. Then he turned and said, "Pity about the crater."

"Will we be allowed inside?" he asked, gesturing to the wreckage.

Haus nodded. "The police have completed their initial inspection and were politely told not to come back. And I ensured the media was escorted out in a similar fashion. You'll be alone to do your detecting and have full access."

Dylan adjusted her coat and motioned toward the doors. "Then let's get started."

They walked together up the wide steps. Despite the modern reconstruction, the structure still bore the bones of its former life. There were arched doorways, heavy wooden beams, stained-glass windows long since reinforced with security polymer. It was a place caught between its past sanctity and its current science.

Inside, the air was cool and sterile. A receptionist sat behind a bulletproof glass desk. Armed guards stood discreetly at the hallway intersections. Every inch of the building radiated wealth and quiet menace.

Haus turned to them. “Your first interview will be with the director representing the Americas. He’s waiting in the conference chamber.”

Dylan took the lead. “We’ll want to take a look at what’s left of the lab first.”

Chapter Four

The Lab

The trio ascended two flights of stairs, their shoes clicking against worn marble steps that had once echoed the footsteps of nuns in silent procession. Now, only the occasional creak of metal and fluttering of the tarp overhead broke the still air. At the top of the stairs, they passed through a thick sheet of plastic, sealed loosely around the doorframe with duct tape. The smell hit them instantly—char and melted insulation, with a strange, sterile sweetness, like overheated chemicals.

The third-floor lab hallway had been obliterated.

To Dylan, it looked as though a colossal eraser had dragged across a blueprint, wiping out everything in a jagged half-circle. Sunlight poured through the exposed structure where the wall once stood, casting long, crooked shadows across blackened flooring and tangled metal. Half-melted lab benches jutted out from the ruins like broken ribs.

Haus and the detectives paused at the edge of the corridor, surveying the aftermath in solemn silence.

"It looks like something out of a nightmare," Dillon muttered, stepping gingerly toward the blown-out section.

Dylan approached the jagged edge where the floor had sheared away. She crouched, squinting down through the debris. "The blast didn't just take out this floor—it caved in the one below." Her voice was calm, clinical. "From the outside, it must look like a shark took a bite out of the building."

Haus didn't respond. He merely stood there, hands behind his back, jaw set in a way that made Dylan wonder if he ever relaxed.

Dillon turned toward him. "How many were killed?"

"Fourteen," Haus said. "Twelve lab technicians, Director Lutz, and Mr. Iglesia. All fourteen were recovered and identified—some partially—but identified, nonetheless. Their families have been contacted."

"No survivors?" Dillon asked, though he knew the answer.

"Not from this wing," Haus said. "The explosion was... surgical. Brutal but focused. Whoever planted it knew exactly where to place the device for maximum destruction."

"Did the police determine what kind of explosive it was?" Dylan asked, brushing her fingers against a heat-warped metal support beam.

Haus nodded. "Plastic explosive. Possibly C-4 or something similar. Sophisticated. The explosive was just enough to take out this section of the building without collapsing the whole structure."

"And the lab?" Dylan turned back to him, eyebrows raised. "What kind of research was being done here?"

Haus allowed himself a small, bitter smile. "That's the strangest part. No one really knows. Not even me. The lab operated under full confidentiality. The personnel were forbidden from discussing their work, even with family. Whatever they were doing here was kept strictly off the record."

Dillon crossed his arms, clearly skeptical. "So, you're telling me not even Lutz or Iglesia kept notes? Reports? Nothing?"

“You’d think so,” Haus said. “But no. No documentation has been found. No cloud backups, no external servers. If they had hard copies, they would be incinerated. The secret of this lab died with them.”

Dylan shook her head, still scanning the wreckage. “We’re not going to find anything useful up here. The blast wiped it all clean. I assume there’s more you can show us?”

Haus inclined his head. “Yes. We have camera footage from the lab's security system. Captured everything up until the moment of the explosion.”

“Then please take us there. Now.” Dylan’s tone was sharp. “And if there’s anything else you’re reluctant to share, I suggest you reconsider.”

Without another word, Haus turned and led them back down the back stairwell, this time skipping steps like a man in a hurry. The hallway they entered was lined with utility doors and exposed piping. At the end stood a thick, steel-reinforced door marked “SECURITY.”

Inside, a lone security officer sat at a console, eyes glazed as he watched live camera feeds tick across a single monitor. The room smelled faintly of coffee and ozone.

Haus gestured at the screen. “Show them the recording—just before the explosion.”

The officer nodded, tapped a few keys, and the screen flickered. Moments later, the surveillance footage began to play.

Multiple angles filled the screen—hallways, workspaces, closets. Technicians moved briskly, focused on their tasks. Laughter echoed faintly through one corridor. Then, at the center of the footage, two men appeared—walking side by side down the main hall on the third floor.

"There." Haus pointed. "That's Iglesia and Director Lutz."

The camera followed them as they moved down the hall, engaged in animated conversation. Lutz gestured toward a large room at the end. Iglesia nodded, peering inside. Then, abruptly, he turned away from the door and headed toward the emergency fire exit.

Lutz hesitated, then hurried after him.

The screen went white. Static filled the room.

Dillon leaned forward. "That was it?"

"Yes," said Haus. "A digital forensics team analyzed the footage frame by frame. The explosion occurred just as they reached the exit. The blast originated to the left of the large room. Beyond that, nothing is usable."

Dylan frowned. "Did the footage reveal anything odd—anyone lurking, carrying equipment, maybe accessing restricted areas?"

Haus shook his head. "We reviewed all the feeds. No suspicious activity. No unauthorized personnel in the area. Just... nothing."

Dylan stepped back from the console, arms crossed, deep in thought. "So you brought us in because you're out of leads. You've hit a wall."

Haus hesitated, then nodded, the mask slipping. "Yes. And the optics are bad. If we can't identify the perpetrator or motive, it reflects weakness. Especially after losing one of our directors."

"Well," Dylan said, softening just slightly. "You were smart to call us. Let's see what we can do."

Dillon watched her for a beat, then turned back to the screen. "Can we rewind again? Just before the explosion. A few seconds earlier. Slow it down."

The officer did as instructed, and they watched once more. Iglesia stops. Lutz catches up. Iglesia turns toward the fire exit.

"Stop there," Dylan said. "Now frame by frame."

Lutz moved ahead of Iglesia, almost blocking his path. Then Iglesia stepped by him. A flicker on the wall caught Dylan's eye.

"There." She pointed. "What's that—on the wall next to the fire exit?"

Haus leaned closer. "That's the firebox—holds the ax and hose reel. Standard issue. Old building code."

Dylan was already out the door.

They followed her back up the stairs, pushing through the tarp once more. She strode purposefully to the ruined section of the corridor and stopped in front of the charred remains of the wall-mounted firebox.

It was still mostly intact—blackened, melted in places, but recognizable. The glass had been blown out. The ax was missing.

Dillon stepped up beside her. "I'm looking, but nothing odd's jumping out at me."

Dylan didn't answer. Her mind was already turning over possibilities.

"This," she muttered, "is where it happened."

"You're thinking the bomb was in the firebox?" Haus asked.

She shook her head. "No. I'm thinking... the ax."

"The ax?"

"What if it wasn't there for emergencies? What if it were swapped? Or rigged?"

Dillon followed her train of thought. "A concealed device, maybe triggered when the box was disturbed?"

"Or when someone opened the door." Dylan knelt beside the frame, running a gloved hand over the metal casing. "See this hinge? It's newer than the rest of the mount. Maybe it was tampered with."

Haus looked shaken. "But why would Iglesia or Lutz open it?"

"Maybe they didn't," Dylan said. "Maybe someone else did earlier. Or maybe..."

She paused. A memory tugged at the edge of her thoughts. "Back in the footage, Iglesia turns toward the fire exit—and Lutz runs to stop him. What if Lutz knew?"

"Knew what?" Dillon asked.

"That something was there. He saw him heading toward danger and tried to stop it."

"You think Lutz was trying to protect him?"

"Maybe," Dylan said.

Dillon blinked. "You think Lutz planted the bomb?"

"I don't know yet. But if the trigger was motion-based, or pressure-based, or even timed—" She stopped, brow furrowed. "We need to examine what's left of that firebox. Closely. Maybe even have it sent to a private forensic team."

Haus nodded. "We can arrange that."

Dylan stood up and took a long look down the twisted hall. "There's something here. This wasn't random. Whoever did this knew where to place the device. Knew who would be in the hallway at that exact time."

Dillon added quietly, "And maybe they knew how to make it look like no one ever would."

The wind stirred outside, sending a faint ripple through the tarp behind them. Dylan turned, eyes sharp. "Let's go back downstairs. I want to see what else is in that footage."

Haus hesitated, then said, "Remember, the first regional director is in the conference chamber. He's been waiting, and I'm sure he's ready to be done here."

"Good," Dylan said, striding away from the wreckage. "So are we."

Chapter Five

The Americas

Dylan and Dillon waited inside a sleek, sterile conference room. The walls were floor-to-ceiling glass, offering both transparency and surveillance, a paradox that suited their hosts perfectly. There was a subtle hum in the air from hidden ventilation, and the faint scent of antiseptic lingered, as if the room had been wiped down minutes before their arrival.

At the center of the glossy black conference table sat a multi-port streaming camera system, its lenses blinking intermittently like a watchful insect. Dillon raised a brow and gestured to the setup. “You think they’re expecting a show?”

Dylan shrugged, folding her arms. “If so, we’re the entertainment.”

Before Dillon could reply, the door opened and a youngish man in a tailored blazer strolled in with the energy of someone used to commanding attention.

“Ah, you’re finally here! I was in this room first, but decided to use the restroom when I heard you were touring the lab. You won’t be needing the streaming gear today,” he said with a grin, waving a hand toward the camera as if dismissing a household pet. “But don’t worry, there are always security cameras watching. Always.” He stepped forward briskly, offering a firm handshake first to Dylan, then to Dillon. “Call me Mr. Barn. My apologies in advance; we all have code names. Ridiculous, I know.”

Dillon and Dylan exchanged brief glances. The charm was palpable but practiced.

"Yes, we've already met Mr. Church and Mr. Haus," Dylan said evenly, taking the handshake without rising from her chair.

"Then I'll skip the formalities," Barn said, slipping into the chair across from them. "Tragic, what happened to Iglesia. No one saw that coming. He didn't deserve that kind of exit."

"You're right," Dylan replied. "No one deserves to be blown up in their workplace. But someone made that decision. Someone who knew exactly what they were doing."

Barn raised his hands slightly. "Let me be upfront. There's no animosity between us. Zero. We're all part of the same ecosystem. When one of us prospers, we all do. Each region contributes its profits into a communal investment pool. Think of it as...a giant syndicate pot. At the end of each fiscal year, we compare gains—purely for bragging rights, nothing more."

Dylan leaned forward, her voice pointed. "Some might say that's *exactly* the motive for murder. Knock out the leader, take the top spot, control the narrative."

Barn chuckled, but it didn't reach his eyes. "You've been watching too many crime dramas. I get it, I really do—those stories need villains, betrayals, power grabs. But that's fiction. We operate differently. We thrive on cooperation, not coups."

Dillon tilted his head. "That almost sounds utopian. Explain."

Barn tapped the table lightly as he thought. "We all rose through the ranks by making our superiors look good. It's a bottom-up culture of performance and loyalty. You don't succeed by stepping on others, but by lifting them up. Anyone who doesn't buy into that ethos is removed—quietly and permanently, but not always violently."

Dylan arched a brow. "So, you're saying no one ever dies on the job?"

Barn paused, then smiled tightly. "People retire young. They cash out, disappear to islands or mountains. We make it easy for them to walk away. Death doesn't factor into our promotions. Iglesia was the exception, not the rule."

"Convenient," Dillon muttered. "Still, Iglesia is dead. That's a fact."

Barn nodded solemnly. "Which is why you're here. The decision to bring in outsiders—*you*—weren't taken lightly. We have our own internal intelligence teams, incredibly effective ones. But Iglesia specifically asked for you. And frankly, we were all curious why. You must've impressed him."

"We owe him," Dylan said quietly. "He did us a favor."

Barn corrected her gently. "He left you a fortune from that sample cruise ship job. He didn't have to do that. You showed him something rare—intellect, ingenuity, and foresight. The truth is, we admired his decision. The Syndicate *never* gives money away, especially not to outsiders. But he insisted."

Dillon cut in, studying Barn carefully. "So let's cut to it. Did you kill him?"

Barn didn't flinch. "No."

His answer was immediate, flat, and unblinking. No twitch, no subtle tick. Even Dylan, who had developed a second sense for lies, couldn't read anything off him.

"Do you know who did?" she asked, watching even more closely.

"No."

Again, nothing. Not even the typical micro expressions—nostril flare, lip compression, shifting eyes.

Barn leaned forward. “Let me offer some context. Iglesia and I came up around the same time. Different tracks, same ladder. He took over the European region, I took the Americas.”

“And what’s your region’s specialty?” Dillon asked.

Barn smiled. “Cannabis.”

Dylan frowned. “Marijuana? Isn’t that mostly legal now?”

“Exactly,” Barn said, almost gleefully. “That’s where the real profit is. You’re thinking like outlaws. We think like entrepreneurs. We saw the shift coming. While others kept fighting for a shrinking illegal market, I turned our operation into a legal juggernaut.”

Dillon narrowed his eyes. “Go on.”

“I bought thousands of acres from Canada to Argentina. Set up cultivation farms, greenhouses, and shipping centers. We seed, we grow, we harvest, we replant. Our agricultural arm is registered, our stocks are public, and our boardrooms have more lawyers than guns.”

Dylan tilted her head, intrigued despite herself. “So, you’re legal drug lords?”

“Essentially,” Barn said with a smirk. “Imagine this: all those baby boomers who were stoners in the sixties? Now they’re in their seventies—with disposable income. They don’t just want *premium*, boutique strains. Edibles. Oils. Pills. We market relaxation, nostalgia, and even spirituality. And we’re the only ones who can scale fast enough to meet demand.”

Dillon glanced at Dylan. “Still not sure how this ties back to Iglesia.”

Barn's smile faded. "We had a side deal. Quiet. I was going to use his shipping connections to move container-loads of cannabis into Europe. Controlled quantities, of course—test runs. If it worked, we'd scale. Split the end-of-year tabulation bonuses."

"So, what went wrong?" Dylan asked.

"I don't know." Barn looked genuinely troubled. "We were about to finalize the third run. Iglesia had the clients. I had the product. Then boom—literally."

Dillon leaned back, chewing the inside of his cheek. "Could someone have caught wind of your side hustle and decided to end it?"

"Maybe," Barn admitted. "But the profits would have benefited both regions. And everyone else in the Syndicate. It wasn't against the rules."

"But maybe someone thought it crossed a line," Dylan suggested. "Or maybe someone didn't like how close you two were getting."

Barn sighed and checked his watch again. "Possibly. But speculation isn't evidence. And I'm out of time."

He stood, adjusting his blazer. "Look, if you need anything else, don't hesitate. Really. Ask anything, any time. But my official window is closed."

With a quick nod, he exited, his footsteps crisp on the polished floor.

Dylan waited until she was sure the door had shut, then turned her face subtly away from the ceiling camera.

"What do you think?" she whispered.

Dillon sighed, eyes still on the empty chair Barn had vacated. "I kind of hope they're not all like Mr. Barn."

“Yeah,” Dylan muttered. “Too clean. Too smooth.”

Dillon rubbed his chin. “Too smart to be sloppy. And bombs are sloppy.”

They both sat in silence for a moment, the quiet hum of the ventilation system suddenly loud in their ears.

“Let’s dig deeper into those shipping manifests,” Dillon said finally. “I want to know exactly where those containers were headed. And who signed off.”

Dylan nodded. “And let’s find out who benefits the most from Iglesia’s absence.”

They stood in unison, moving as a single unit toward the door, already thinking three steps ahead. Whoever killed Iglesia had started a ripple in a sea of sharks. The trick would be finding one with blood on its teeth.

Chapter Six

Northern Asia

"May I sit down? Also, and for your information, I am fluent in many languages, but I will use English. Is that all right?"

Dylan and Dillon stood briefly out of respect and answered in unison as they returned to their seats. "Yes, of course."

The man before them looked younger than the others they'd met so far—sharp suit, impossibly polished shoes, and a voice that hummed with a confident calm. His every move felt calculated, but not robotic. He was a man used to having control and not giving an inch more than necessary.

"You may call me Mr. Bank," he said. "And before you even ask, I did not kill Iglesia."

Dylan tilted her head. "We understand you represent Northern Asia."

"Yes. It's mostly Russia and China," Bank said smoothly, folding his hands together on the table. "Two countries with a shared history of tension and opportunity. It's a region of contrast. Old power meets new money. And behind the curtain? Us."

"What can you tell us about—"

Mr. Bank abruptly sat forward, cutting off Dillon without hesitation. "Though the others might tell you differently, everybody hated Iglesia. I hated Iglesia. Mr. High and mighty. Mr. Suave. We all came up through the ranks the same way, but he thought he was something else. He believed he was better than the rest of us. Smarter. Nobler. More sophisticated. And maybe he was—but he made damn sure we knew it."

He leaned back slightly, smirking. "Well, now he's dead. And no, I won't miss him, and I won't mourn him."

The detectives exchanged a glance. Rarely did a suspect—or person of interest—open with contempt so freely. It was almost too clean. Too intentional. Mr. Bank wasn't just unloading; he was directing the narrative.

Mr. Bank continued. "Let me guess—Mr. Barn told you the opposite. That Iglesia was beloved. That we all respected him. That he was some kind of Robin Hood with stock options." He gave a short, mirthless laugh. "Why, even the codename he gave himself—Mr. Church—reeks of sanctimony. Regal, divine. As if he were our savior."

"He certainly had a reputation for elegance," Dylan said carefully. "You said you came up through the ranks together?"

"Yes. Side by side for the better part of a decade. Though we ended up in different regions, we began as couriers and junior analysts in the same European pipeline. The irony of it all—it's stunning."

"What irony?" Dillon asked, leaning forward slightly.

Bank's tone softened, almost reflective. "You probably don't know his origin story. It's tragic, really. His father fell in with some dangerous people—real brutes. Iglesia was sitting in the car outside his school while his father went inside to collect his siblings. A bomb, meant for the father, went off and killed everyone inside the school. Iglesia watched it all."

A moment passed before Dillon said quietly, "We didn't know any of that."

"No. Few people do. He kept it close. But it shaped him. It made him determined—obsessed, even—with control. Order. He thought if he could plan every detail, nothing would ever go wrong again." Mr. Bank's voice turned brittle. "Of course, life doesn't work that way. A bomb doesn't care about your plans."

Dylan adjusted in her seat, steering things forward. "Let's talk about your region."

"Northern Asia is the heart of tech," Bank said, straightening. "We own infrastructure—fiber optics, chip manufacturers, energy contracts. We control major data centers, and yes, we're involved in both hacking operations and their countermeasures. Cybersecurity firms? Ours. Ransomware teams? Ours. We profit from the breach *and* the cure. It's elegant. Dual-sided revenue streams."

"And profitable?" Dillon asked, already knowing the answer.

"Consistently second place in the year-end tallies," Bank said, his jaw tightening. "Guess who was always first."

Dylan didn't need to say it.

"Iglesia," Bank spat. "With his private equity plays, black-market art trades, high-seas piracy, and whatever new lab venture he was throwing his weight behind. The man had an uncanny knack for being ahead of the curve. He called it vision. I called it arrogance."

"He had a new project?" Dillon asked.

Bank hesitated. "He'd started this lab. Said it was going to revolutionize our revenue model. Wouldn't give us specifics, just that it was 'bigger than the cruise ship demo.' He teased the results, talked about AI, about human behavior modeling, and some predictive tech mixed with psychology and biotechnology. It felt... invasive. Like a way to control people, not just markets."

Dylan exchanged another glance with Dillon. “Sounds like a potential motive.”

“You mean for me to kill him?” Mr. Bank asked, raising an eyebrow. “Sure. That’s one way to spin it. But that assumes I think small. Kill the leader to take his spot? That’s not how the Syndicate works. We don’t advance by murder. That’s not our culture. Not anymore.”

“Still, if you felt he was out playing you...” Dillon pushed.

Bank smirked. “Come now. Give me more credit than that. If I wanted him gone, I’d have made sure I *wasn’t* the obvious suspect. No rants. No confessions of dislike. I’d be crying on your shoulder right now with a handful of tissues.”

Dylan shifted in her seat. “Let’s talk about the cruise ship heist. The sample one.”

Bank sighed. “Yes. I opposed letting you two keep the money. Everyone else voted yes. I voted last. I voted no.”

“Why?” Dillon asked.

“Because rules matter. Or they’re supposed to,” Bank said. “We were building a system, one designed to function beyond the old-school mafia dynamics. When you hand out millions to outsiders, you break that system. Sure, you earned Iglesia’s respect, but you also exposed us to risk. I didn’t like it then. I like it even less now.”

“So, you resented him for giving us the money.”

“I resented that he played hunches and favorites,” Bank clarified. “He saw himself as a kingmaker. But I never asked for his crown, and I sure as hell didn’t want to bend the knee.”

Dylan stood. “Thank you for your time, Mr. Bank. We’ll be in touch.”

Mr. Bank stood as well but paused before leaving. “There’s one more thing.”

Dillon waited.

“That sample heist you thwarted? Iglesia took detailed notes. He worked out every kink, every misstep. At our last meeting, he told us he had planned over forty coordinated heists at different airports, ports, railways, and even floating data centers. All within the next year.”

Dylan frowned. “That’s insane. Forty?”

Bank nodded. “And he had teams trained and staged across four continents. Each operation was self-contained. We didn't even know the full extent.”

Dillon’s voice was low. “So, if he was the golden goose...”

“Exactly,” Bank said, stepping to the door. “Everyone here knows: You don’t blow up the golden goose.”

With that, he left them alone in the glass-walled room.

Dylan turned away from the cameras embedded in the corners. “What do you think?”

Dillon leaned back. “I think Mr. Bank is the kind of guy who doesn’t need to lie. If he *had* killed Iglesia, he’d be clever enough to keep his hands clean. Or make it look like someone else did.”

“So, you believe him?” she asked.

“I believe he hated Iglesia,” Dillon replied. “But that might not matter. In a place like this, hate might be the default setting.”

They sat in silence for a moment, digesting the implications. Each interview peeled back another layer of a tangled empire that operated by its own rules—and its own sense of justice.

Whatever was going on inside this syndicate, it was bigger than just one murder.

Chapter Seven

Southern Asia

Dylan and Dillon sat in the now-familiar conference room, waiting. The space was quiet except for the distant hum of recycled air and the muted clink of silverware from somewhere else in the compound. Interviews were starting to run together, and it already felt like they'd been inside the syndicate's fortress for their week.

Finally, the door clicked open.

A woman entered briskly, no bodyguards, no entourage. Her features were calm, her expression unreadable. She looked utterly unremarkable—black slacks, a soft white blouse, and long black hair pulled loosely over one shoulder. The only thing animated about her was her hand, which immediately went to a small silver necklace she began twirling with quick, nervous fingers.

"Hello," she said, nodding curtly. "Sorry for being five minutes late. I was on a long-distance call." More necklace twirling. Her voice was steady, but something in her eyes flickered with tension.

"My code name is Ms. School," she said, with the faintest smile. "But please... just call me School."

Dillon offered a practiced, disarming nod. "Of course. Tell us a little about yourself."

"Well, like everyone else at my level, I worked myself up. No shortcuts. I started as a smuggler, just moving goods—rare seeds, small electronics, precious metals—across borders in South Asia."

She paused to smooth a wrinkle from her sleeve. "But over time, I discovered my strength wasn't in moving things. It was moving people."

Dylan tensed. She already didn't like where this was going.

"I'm in the Southern Asia region," School continued. "My piece of the pie is trafficking."

Dylan's eyebrows knit together in shock. She sat back, jaw tensing.

School noticed. "No. Not like that. Not anymore," she said quickly, still spinning her necklace. "Trafficking used to mean the worst things imaginable. Underage kids, sex trades, abuse. It was barbaric. But I'm very proud to say I pioneered a new way."

Dillon raised an eyebrow, his voice low. "Trafficking still seems... bad."

"Yes, well... maybe," she admitted, slowing her spinning fingers. "But also, very profitable. And not just for us."

Dylan leaned forward, arms crossed. "You're saying you've *improved* trafficking?"

School's fingers went still on her necklace. "I broker deals for large groups of people—some of them children, yes—to work for their new hosts or owners for a contract period of five years. After that, they're free to go. We provide them with legal documentation, housing, job training, and a modest exit payment. It's regulated by us. Safer. Cleaner."

Dylan looked horrified. "That sounds like indentured servitude with extra paperwork."

School didn't flinch. "Maybe it is. But do you know what the alternative is for these people? Starvation. Disease. Generations of nothingness. I offer them a way out. A five-year trade for a lifetime of potential. I don't see myself as a trafficker of bodies—I see myself as a trafficker of *hope*."

The detectives stared at her in stunned silence. To her, this was moral calculus. To them, it felt like moral corrosion with better branding.

Dylan half-stood before catching herself. "You can spin it however you want, but—"

"We're not here to pass judgment," Dillon interjected firmly, shooting her a glance. "We're here to solve a murder."

Ms. School's hands dropped from the necklace, finally still. She leaned forward, her expression suddenly serious.

"I certainly didn't kill Iglesia. And if I had... I wouldn't be sitting here, speaking to you."

"Do you know who did?" Dillon asked, watching her closely.

"I don't," she said, shaking her head. "But I have a guess."

That caught their attention.

"It has to be his wife," she said plainly. "Vyra."

There was a long pause.

Dylan blinked. "Vyra?"

Ms. School nodded. "Yes. She's the only spouse. All of us other directors, every single one of us, are single. That's by design. The life we lead, the power we control, it doesn't mix well with marriage. But Iglesia married her anyway. We all raised our eyebrows, but no one dared challenge him."

"Why her?" Dillon asked. "What's special about Vyra?"

School gave a knowing smile. "Have either of you seen her?"

"No," Dylan said. "She's scheduled after the Africa rep."

"Then you'll understand when you do," School said cryptically. "But let me change gears and talk about the motive. You want a motive? Here it is: Syndicate protocol states that when a member dies, their spouse inherits their territory. Instantly. No apprenticeship. No loyalty trials. No vetting. Vyra would go from being an outsider to the most powerful woman in our system in one move."

Dylan gasped. "So, you're saying..."

"I'm saying she didn't have to claw her way through the muck like the rest of us. All she had to do was wait. Or maybe... not wait."

Dillon folded his arms. "You're right, of course. That's a strong motive. But... It seems too obvious. Wouldn't she know she'd be the first suspect?"

"She's not stupid," School agreed. "But love makes people do stupid things. Or maybe ambition does. Honestly, with Vyra, it's hard to tell the difference."

"And you think lawyer Haus already checked everyone's alibis?" Dillon asked.

"Definitely. He's thorough. But we all know an alibi can be arranged if you have enough time and money." She pushed her chair back. "Anyway. That's all I've got. I've stayed five minutes longer than I intended."

She stood abruptly. Dillon followed suit.

"You've been most helpful," he said.

Ms. School gave a tight smile, her fingers already drifting back to the necklace. "Good luck, detectives. I think you're going to need it."

Once the door clicked shut behind her, Dylan turned to Dillon.

"She's our first real lead," she said, barely able to keep her voice down. "Vyra. Think about it. No one had more to gain. And she probably has the money, the reach, and the brains to hire someone to blow up the lab with Iglesia inside. She could've been halfway around the world sipping champagne when the fireball went up."

Dillon remained quiet, brows furrowed.

"She's perfect," Dylan went on. "Not everyone suspects the grieving widow. And the second she's installed in his seat, the investigation starts falling apart. Nobody questions her authority. You know the phrase, 'Follow the money'? Well, we're about to meet the end of the trail."

Dillon finally spoke. "I guess that's one theory."

Dylan looked incredulous. "One theory? It's practically a signed confession! She's the only outsider with an insider's reward."

Dillon's eyes narrowed slightly. "Don't you think that's *too* perfect?"

"What do you mean?"

"My intuition is on high alert. I mean… when everything lines up *this* neatly, it usually means someone wanted it to."

Dylan hesitated.

"What if we're being pushed toward her?" he said, his voice low. "What if someone inside the board is pointing the blame away from themselves and toward the one person who can't defend herself yet?"

Dylan was quiet for a long time. "Maybe. But it still makes sense. The system is built so that Vyra benefits the second he dies. That's not just a motive; it's a built-in reward."

"It's also a setup," Dillon said. "And setups make great endings. But they also make great red herrings."

Dylan crossed her arms. "Don't you see? It's the perfect crime. Everyone suspects her because this time—this *one* time—they're actually right."

Dillon sighed, looking at the ceiling as if trying to find answers written in the tiles. "But that doesn't leave any room for a final twist."

Dylan smirked and rolled her eyes. "You and your twists."

He looked back at her, deadly serious. "We're in a room full of people who run the world's underworld. There's *always* a twist."

Chapter Eight

Africa

The sound of heavy, deliberate footsteps echoed down the marble corridor.

Dylan and Dillon turned toward the noise, watching as a tall and imposing man approached the conference room. He moved with a certain authority—not the rushed pace of a lackey or the slouch of someone weighed down by guilt. This man owned his space.

He was massive—not just in height, but in presence. His frame filled the doorway like a stone monolith. Broad shoulders pressed against the limits of his tailored suit, and a weathered but regal face studied the detectives as he entered.

“I'm Museum—ah, I mean, Mr. Museum,” he corrected himself with a deep, gravelly voice. His accent hinted at a pan-African upbringing, the kind formed by elite international schools and diplomatic dinners. “I represent all of Africa.”

He walked to the opposite end of the long glass table, each step slow and deliberate. With a slight groan, he settled into a chair that barely seemed large enough for him. It creaked in protest.

“I understand you've been invited here to solve the lab bombing.”

Dillon nodded. “Yes. We've been conducting interviews with the board, asking respectfully if anyone had a motive to kill Mr. Iglesia.”

Museum raised an eyebrow, then gave a small laugh. “Don't you mean to ask if I killed him?”

Dillon met his gaze calmly. "I guess, yes, that's part of it."

"Then let me put it to rest. I did not kill Iglesia, nor do I know anyone who would." He adjusted in his seat, still sizing them up like one might appraise art or cattle. "And if that's the extent of your interrogation, I'll be leaving."

Dylan stood, trying to sound both respectful and insistent. "Before you go, could you briefly share what profitable endeavors the African region is currently contributing to the Syndicate?"

Museum paused. Something flickered in his eyes—either irritation or curiosity—and then he leaned back slowly.

"The African strategy is all about land. Ownership, control, development. I've spent the last decade buying up enormous tracts of undeveloped or underutilized land. Entire provinces, in some cases. Places where no one else was looking. That's where the real future lies."

Dylan tilted her head. "How does that generate any annual profits?"

"It's simple," he said. "We don't just buy land—we transform it. We build cities from scratch. Smart cities. Tech hubs. We take dusty border towns and convert them into thriving metropolises. We own construction companies, the material suppliers, and the electrical grid contracts. Every piece of it."

"None of that seems particularly illegal," Dillon remarked.

Museum gave a short, satisfied smile. "It's not. In fact, it's quite the opposite. We operate under national and international law. We grease the right palms, of course—nothing gets done otherwise—but all our papers are clean. One of our most lucrative ventures is in airport infrastructure. Do you know how many new regional airports are being built across Africa right now?"

Dillon shook his head.

"Thirty-seven. And every single one of them was orchestrated by my division. After construction, we lease the rights to airline carriers for a hundred years. Think about that. A century of guaranteed income. It's slow money, not fast, but it's permanent. Legacy money."

Dylan was taking notes, frowning slightly. "So, you're more of a long-term investor than a short-term profiteer."

Museum nodded. "Exactly. My vision is to eventually make the Syndicate fully legitimate. No shadows. No crime at all. Just wealth and power. We've already got the infrastructure."

Dillon leaned forward. "That's quite the transformation—from crime syndicate to corporate empire."

"You'd be surprised how thin that line really is," Museum said, almost wistfully. "Some of our enemies still think like petty criminals. Guns, drugs, backroom deals. That era is dying. The future is contracts, land deeds, corporate control. *Soft power.*"

Dylan looked up from her notebook. "Do you know what was happening in the lab before the explosion?"

Museum's expression didn't change, but there was a glint of something—curiosity, maybe, or resentment. "At last month's board meeting, Iglesia told us he was on the verge of announcing a new revenue stream. One that would supposedly double the Syndicate's global profits within a year."

"Double?" Dillon repeated, surprised. "That's huge."

Museum nodded. "He was always ambitious. But he was also secretive. He didn't say what it was, just that he'd reveal it when the time was right."

Dylan saw an opening and took it. "And did that make you mad? Knowing that if he pulled it off, you might never again win the annual regional profit award?"

For the first time, Mr. Museum's calm demeanor cracked. He narrowed his eyes and leaned forward slightly.

"I always thought that competition was idiotic," he said with surprising vehemence. "A popularity contest among billionaires. Pitting us against one another like school children. There was nothing to be gained from it. It encouraged short-term thinking, bad investments, and dangerous risks. I'm building a continent. Do you think I care who wins a trophy?"

Dillon offered a slight, amused smile. "That's a fair point."

Museum stood, slowly. Another low groan escaped him, and both detectives couldn't help but glance at his knee as it stiffened awkwardly.

"This?" he said, noticing. "Old sports injury. Rugby. I was a forward."

He took one heavy step toward the door, then paused.

"It's maybe not for me to say," he began, without turning back, "but if I were investigating this situation, I'd be spending a lot less time on these interviews."

Dillon looked up sharply. "What do you mean?"

"You're trying to eliminate one of the directors. That's a noble idea, but misguided. If I were in your position, I would have already assumed it *wasn't* one of us. Too much to lose. Too many eyes on us. I'd be looking at everyone *outside* the inner circle."

He opened the door, but not before leaving one last comment hanging in the air. "You're playing a game of chess, detectives. Just make sure you're not the pawns."

Then he was gone.

The door clicked shut behind him. Silence returned.

Dylan looked at Dillon.

"Well, he's not wrong." They both said it at the same time and then shared a dry smile.

Dillon leaned back in his chair, eyes scanning the ceiling tiles again as if it might help him see the whole puzzle.

"He's got a point. We've been so focused on these board members—trying to sniff out motive, greed, rivalry—but maybe we're too close to the fire to see the smoke."

"But who else would have access to the lab? It's not like any outsider could just stroll in and plant a bomb."

Dillon nodded. "True. But let's think like Museum. Long-term, strategic. If Iglesia really had a way to double profits, that doesn't just affect the board—it affects *everyone* connected to the syndicate. Lower-tier captains, rival cartels, corporate fronts... Hell, even governments that depend on their share of the under-the-table revenue."

Dylan's expression turned thoughtful. "So you're saying the killer might not have been trying to climb the ladder—but to stop someone else from reaching too high."

"Exactly."

She closed her notebook slowly. "We're going to have to widen our scope."

Dillon stood. "Let's finish these interviews. Vyra's next."

Dylan nodded. "Time to meet the widow."

And with that, they unknowingly headed into a brand-new storm.

Chapter Nine

Europe

"Hello. I'm Vyra." The woman walked toward the back of the detectives, who were back in the conference room after a lunch break. Neither detective was ready for this new storm. They both turned around to see who that sultry voice belonged to.

Vyra's next words matched what they saw. "I'm really not bad, I'm just drawn that way. That's one of my all-time favorite lines from the movie *Who Shot Roger Rabbit*."

Slinking toward them was a curvaceous woman, late twenties, with long auburn colored hair. Her tight black cocktail dress revealed every inch, and every inch was in just the right place. A couple of workers passing by stopped dead in their tracks before slowly gathering speed again.

Dylan couldn't help but stare. Stare and judge. Vyra was every man's dream girl: perfect weight, perfect height, and drop-dead good looks. This was a woman who was used to getting her way. She felt herself quickly being drawn into the 'Vyra gravity field'. She wanted to give her partner the benefit of the doubt, but Dillon was already up and was moving to shake hands.

Dillon tried not to fawn as he took her hand. He had experience with cute, good-looking, and even pretty, but this was the very first time he was in the presence of beauty. Still, he saw in her eyes, maybe felt, that this was a woman who didn't miss much. He quickly realized she was sizing him up at the same time he was sizing her up.

Dillon pulled out a chair. "Please have a seat right here next to me. I only have a few questions for you to answer, nothing too hard, believe me."

"Well, that's a shame." Vyra kept holding Dillon's hand all the way to her seat. "I hope the fact that I'm wearing all black doesn't put you off. The fact is, I'm still in mourning. But enough about that." She changed her position and crossed her legs toward him. "By the way, another fun fact, Vyra, my name, well, it means truth." She laughed softly, "So, I guess you won't have to swear me in."

Dylan finished processing the woman in front of her and shook off her brain fog. "It's our understanding that you became director and took over the European region after your husband died."

Vyra was looking directly at Dillon. "Yes, I'm single again."

"Don't take this wrong, but you don't look all that shook up."

"It was a tragedy for sure, but not unexpected in this line of work. Igelsia and I talked about his possible demise and what it would mean for me to move on without him. He wanted to make sure I'd be okay if the worst happened."

Dylan pressed on. "What can you tell us about Igelsia's death?"

"Why, absolutely nothing. I suppose all the other members are convinced that I am the bomber." Vyra took a moment to re-cross her sinewy and long tan legs. She did it slowly for effect. "They're all jealous. I can't help how the Syndicate made its rules. So, yes, I get to take over his region and I instantly get a seat on the Syndicate board of directors." Vyra leaned forward. "What code name should I take? At the moment I'm thinking of Ms. Chalet, but that's just because we are here in Switzerland."

Dillon felt a small out-of-body experience happening. He felt himself observing the conversations rather than being involved with them. He also felt himself scanning Vyra's responses for body language changes or for what he always looked for, the hard swallow. When he came back down to earth, he asked, "How did you two meet?"

"My husband loved to gamble, you know, just a little. He came into a gambling salon in Vegas, where I was working as security. Security used me as a decoy at the gaming tables because no one suspected me of being someone who worked for the casino. Anyway, Igelsia and I locked eyes." She gave a slight chuckle, "I guess you could say he's been my prisoner ever since."

Dylan smirked, "Great. Let's get down to it. He was older than you by at least twenty years." She saw Vyra nod. "Which did you love more, him or his money?"

Vyra's demeanor and tone changed on a dime. "Ok, woman to woman. I'll lay out my life story. From a young age, I had a smokin' hot body and these model looks. I've always used it to my advantage. There's no crime in that. What may surprise you is that I have brains to match. I was way too much for Zumbrota Minnesota. That was briefly my hometown. Do you know it?"

"Can't say I've heard of it."

"Our city slogan is, 'We're the only Zumbrota in the world'." Can you imagine? That was the best slogan they could think of. The population is like three thousand and change. The city is nestled on the north fork of the Zumbro River." Vyra paused to take a breath. "Anyway, there was no way I was going to stay in some 'one red covered bridge town' with no stoplight. I knew I wanted bigger things. I studied and applied myself, and I got a scholarship to Dartmouth. It will probably surprise you, but I have a business degree in management with a minor in statistics. The day I graduated, I made up my mind to skip the corporate ladder and instead marry rich. I guess that brings us up to the present."

Dillon felt compelled to ask, "Did you kill your husband?"

One single tear produced itself out of nowhere and ran down Vyra's face. "I'm not going to dignify that with an answer." Vyra made a show out of getting a handkerchief from her purse and wiping her cheek. "But I will tell you this, I'm considering giving up my syndicate director seat for a small fee. If I were the killer, would I do that?"

This new information threw the detectives for a loop. Dylan regrouped. "What do you know of your late husband's business here in the lab?"

"Almost nothing. He kept me in the dark about the lab. For all I know he was synthesizing some kind of wonder drug."

"Did he get any threats? If it wasn't you, do you have a guess who the real bomber is?"

Vyra was up and out of her chair. "Ok, I'll play detective." She began pacing slowly. "For sure, whoever it is wanted Igelsia dead. They knew exactly where he would be and exactly what time. I've met the other directors only briefly, but my money's on one of them."

"How so?"

"Well, it was no secret that they all hated him for winning the Syndicate's most profitable trophy each year. So, I don't know the bomber's motive for sure, but each director had the means and opportunity."

Dylan had had enough. She rose and pronounced, "That's all for now. We'll let you know if we have any other follow-up questions."

Vyra was not used to being dismissed. She certainly didn't care about it. She stood and made a short show of making sure everything was in its place and moved toward the conference room door. "Well, I hope I've been a little bit helpful..."

Dillon was up in a flash and offered himself as an escort. "You've been very obliging, and we appreciate your time." She paused, and he opened the door.

He went to rejoin Dylan, but she was also on the move. She began her own pacing.

"I don't like her, not at all."

"Shocker!"

Dylan stopped dead in her tracks and glared at her partner. "What's that supposed to mean?" She turned and plopped into the nearest chair.

"Nothing. Nothing at all." He sat down next to her at the conference room table and pretended to look at his phone. The silence continued for quite some time.

Chapter Ten

Liam

Both detectives continued to sit in silence, their faces partially lit by the glow of their phones. Texts, news alerts, and updates scrolled past their eyes as they took a moment after the morning's interviews.

Dillon appreciated the lull. “This is the first time I’ve felt still in hours,” he muttered, rubbing the bridge of his nose.

Dylan didn’t respond. She stood and began pacing slowly around the perimeter of the room, her shoes clicking faintly against the hardwood floor.

“I think it’s time we review our impressions of the suspects we’ve talked to,” she said, more to herself than to Dillon. “Let’s start with—”

The door flew open.

Mr. Haus entered like a gust of wind. His thin frame seemed energized by caffeine or pure adrenaline.

“Are you both finished with the interviews? Excellent. I’d love to hear your thoughts.”

The detectives exchanged a look. No words were needed. Dillon gave a barely perceptible nod. Sure, why not?

Before they could speak, Haus launched into his next thought. “Oh, and some more new information for you. I’ve compiled a list of everyone who died in the lab bombing. Names, titles, last known locations.”

Dillon straightened. "That's helpful. Thanks."

But Haus wasn't finished.

"I've also made a list of all the up-and-comers—candidates who could replace any of the regional directors should a seat open. Based on financials, influence, and profit performance rankings."

Dylan looked up, eyebrows raised. "You're thorough."

"There's more," Haus said, brimming with anticipation. "I took the liberty of collecting and summarizing their recent emails and social media posts. Keywords, sentiment analysis, suspicious communications—all organized and categorized. I just sent you the summary."

Both detectives opened their inboxes. Dylan's eyes widened as she scrolled. Thirty attachments.

Dillon exhaled deeply. "Look, I don't mean to be rude, but could we skip reading through all of this? I assume you're eager to share the highlights."

Haus nodded enthusiastically. "Yes, of course. I'll cut to the chase. Most of it is unremarkable, but two people stood out. The first is the director of the lab—Mr. Lutz. His search history was flooded with inquiries about patent law. He was researching the process of filing for intellectual property rights, particularly for biotechnology. Dozens of articles, forums, and grant reports. You name it."

Dylan frowned. "Sounds like someone planning to strike out on their own."

"Possibly," Haus said. "The second name you'll want to remember is Germandt. He was Iglesia's second-in-command. His digital footprint is... interesting. A good chunk of his private emails were to Vyra."

Dillon raised an eyebrow. "As in Iglesia's widow?"

"Yes," Haus confirmed, his face coloring slightly. "The messages are vague—nothing explicit—but the tone and timing suggest a possible romantic relationship."

Dylan was still pacing. "Well, I'm sure you've seen that she's a big flirt." She started scrolling through Germandt's folder as she lapped the room. "You're right. These read a little like innuendos... cautious ones."

She clicked through the final exchanges. "Ah. Here it is. The most recent message. It's short—and final. Vyra ended it."

Dillon stood and stretched, cracking his neck. He moved to a different chair across the table and dropped into it. "Well, that grape died on the vine." He heaved a sigh and then began. "I'll start with our impressions, if that's okay," he said, eyeing Dylan. "But first...Dylan, can you stop with the track meet?"

Dylan smirked. "Sure." She slid into the seat opposite him and opened her notes. "But I'll go first."

She cleared her throat. "Mr. Barn from the Americas was upbeat and optimistic. He didn't want to believe another director was behind the bombing. Almost too trusting, if you ask me. Mr. Bank, representing northern Asia, was the opposite. Cold. Dismissive. He told us he was glad Iglesia was dead."

Dillon nodded. "Yeah, I got that."

"Ms. School from southern Asia was visibly nervous. She didn't like that Vyra was going to replace Iglesia. She felt undermined, maybe even threatened. Mr. Museum, director of Africa, came off as a long-term thinker. He claimed not to care about the profit competition and said we were wasting our time interviewing board members at all. He may have a point."

"And Vyra?" Mr. Haus asked.

Dylan paused. "She was composed, polite, but there's a storm under the surface. She's grieving a little, sure, but there's something performative about it."

Just then, Dylan's phone vibrated. She glanced down—and froze.

The blood drained from her face.

She stood abruptly. "It's... I have to take this. Be right back." She stepped quickly into the hallway, leaving Dillon and Haus mid-discussion.

As soon as she was out of earshot, Dylan called the office back in Daytona Beach.

The line rang twice before Liberty picked up. "Hello, Dylan and Dillon Investigations."

"It's me," Dylan said, trying to keep her voice steady. "Everything under control over there?"

"Oh, sure," Liberty replied. "Mostly inquiries about our rates. A few new prospects, but they drop off once I mention your minimum retainer. I sorted through the mail and paid the bills."

Dylan smiled faintly. "Glad to hear it. Any personal messages?"

There was a pause. "Yes, actually. One. From two days ago. Some guy called in—left a message and asked me to write it down and make sure you got it."

"Go on," Dylan said, tension rising.

"He said, 'It's Liam. Please call me.'"

Dylan felt her pulse spike.

Liberty continued, "It wasn't a name I recognized, so I didn't think it was urgent. He said he was an old friend and asked where you were."

"And you told him?"

"Sure, I didn't think there was any harm. Did I mess that up?"

"No," Dylan said, closing her eyes. "You're fine. Don't worry about it. Just... let me know if he calls again."

"Of course." Liberty didn't want to intrude but felt compelled, "Who is he anyway?" The line had already gone dead.

Dylan abruptly ended the call and stood motionless in the hallway. Her thumb hovered over the text again.

Liam.

She found an empty conference room nearby and stepped inside. The lights were off, but she didn't bother turning them on. She stared down at the message, heart pounding.

Liam.

Her ex-fiancé.

It had been almost a year. He ended their engagement with cold finality, despite everything they'd built together. Then, months later, she saw him on her Facebook feed—married. Some woman he'd met just a short time prior. Dylan never understood how he moved on so fast. Or why he left out at all.

Her phone buzzed again.

Liam calling.

Her breath caught.

She answered.

“What do you want?” she said, her voice hard.

“Dylan,” Liam said softly. His voice was familiar. Calm. Sure. “I want you back, baby.”

Dylan shut her eyes. The flood of old wounds, regret, rage, and longing hit all at once.

“You don’t get to call me that, and you sure don’t get to say that to me,” she said quietly.

“I know,” he replied. “I know I screwed up. But I can’t stop thinking about you. About us. I made a mistake.”

She was silent for a moment, then sat down slowly.

“I’m working a case,” she said flatly. “Out of the country. And you’re married.”

“I know,” he said. “That’s why I had to call. Before you disappear again. Just... tell me you’ll come meet with me.”

Dylan didn’t respond. She looked out the window at the snow-covered city, her reflection barely visible in the glass.

“I have to go,” she said at last.

“Dylan—”

“Don’t call this number again. Not until I decide if I want to hear from you.”

Liam tried one last time to sell himself. “I’ve made a mistake, a big one. I rushed into my marriage. It didn’t take long at all to see she wasn’t right for me. She just wasn’t you.” He took a quick breath. “I flew all this way. Say you’ll meet me today, this afternoon for a drink.”

She hung up.

Outside the room, the world turned as usual—but inside, everything fell still.

She pressed her forehead to the cold glass and whispered, to no one in particular, “Why now?”

After a few minutes, she stood, squared her shoulders, and reentered the main room, face composed.

“Everything alright?” Dillon asked.

“Let’s get back to work,” Dylan replied, her voice smooth as ice. “I think we’re close.”

Chapter Eleven

It's a Date

Dylan was off in a chair at the far end of the conference table. Dillon and Haus had wrapped up their discussion. Dillon stood, brushing invisible lint from his jacket and gesturing toward the door. "Mr. Haus, you've been most helpful. We'll get back to you as soon as we know something solid."

Mr. Haus tilted his head, his lips tightening. "Bye for now, then. Just a reminder—your one-week deadline is approaching *very* fast." His tone lingered like a warning in the air, souring the room.

After Dillon had walked Mr. Haus out into the hallway, he turned and almost collided with someone standing silently behind him—a small, sharply dressed man with the kind of muscular build that suggested he could break bones as easily as he tied a necktie.

Dillon took an instinctive half-step back. "Whoa. Didn't hear there."

The man didn't flinch. "My name is Germandt. I am an associate of Ms. Vyra. She cordially invites you to join her for a scenic train ride." His accent was clipped, European, his suit custom-fitted. His presence was unmistakably intentional: he wasn't here for small talk, and he wasn't leaving without an answer.

Before Dillon could respond, the conference room door creaked open. Dylan looked out, eyes lowered, her complexion pale and unsettled. The tension in her shoulders spoke volumes.

Dillon's focus shifted. He raised a hand to Germandt. "Give us a moment, will you?" He ushered the man down the hall. He then stepped into the conference room and closed the door firmly before turning to Dylan.

He walked closer. "You look like you've just seen a ghost."

Dylan leaned against the edge of the table. "Do you remember my meltdown about my ex-fiancé? On the cruise ship, during that first case?"

"Liam, right? The guy you found out got remarried?" Dillon's brow furrowed. "Don't tell me..."

"He's here," she whispered. "In Zurich. And he wants to see me. Today."

Dillon's stomach clenched. He hadn't expected that. He knew the name Liam well—it had become a symbol of everything that haunted Dylan's past. But he hadn't expected the man to step out of memory and into their present.

"Are you going to do it?" he asked, trying—and failing—to keep the edge out of his voice.

She looked up, her eyes glassy. "He flew all this way."

Dillon turned away, jaw tight. His thoughts scrambled, battling emotion with reason, but emotion was winning. "How did you even find out he was here? Wait—don't answer that. I can't believe you'd even consider this. After what he did to you?"

"He said he made a mistake," she replied softly. "He rushed into his current marriage. Said she wasn't right for him. That *they* weren't right together."

Dillon shook his head in disbelief. "Didn't he say the *exact same kind of thing* to you when he ended it?"

Dylan winced like he'd hit her. "I wish I hadn't told you so much about him that night."

"Well, you *did*," he snapped. "And I can't unhear it. He shattered you. You were *wrecked.* And now he shows up like some lost puppy, and you're just... what? Thinking about giving him another shot?"

Her eyes flared. "He said he misses me. He said he wants to try again. He wants to know if I could ever forgive him."

Dillon turned to the window, as if the view of the lower Alps might help him center himself. "So, what, you get back together and just forget everything? And what does that mean for us? For our business?"

"I don't know," she said, frustrated. "I can't think about that right now. This is personal."

Dillon turned slowly to face her, his voice low and wounded. "Yeah. Got it. It's personal. I'm just your business partner. I don't get a say."

She crossed her arms, defensive now. "That's not what I meant."

He didn't let her clarify. "Message received." He walked to the conference room door and yanked it open. "Go. I've got something else to do. Catch you in the morning."

Dylan stood motionless for a beat, then gathered her phone and bag and stepped out into the hallway and took a sharp left.

As she walked away, she heard Dillon's voice rise behind her. "Yes, tell Vyra it's a date."

She stopped mid-step and whirled around. "Wow. *Really?* Real mature."

Dillon stood just outside the doorway, his jaw set. Germandt was already halfway down the hall, presumably off to report the success of his errand.

"You stay out of *my* personal life, too," Dillon shot back. "And what did you expect? You drop that bomb about Liam and I'm just supposed to smile and wave?"

Dylan stormed back toward him, heat flushing her cheeks. "What's happening between us—this weird, unspoken *thing*—I don't want it if it's going to be some safe, slow-burn, almost-romance." She pointed at him with every word. "I want fireworks. I want to be *chased.* I want passion, and I want to fall—hard."

He raised a hand. "Stop. Just stop. I don't need the long version."

"No," she said, pushing past his interruption. "You flirt with me when it's convenient. You like the safety of this... this proximity. But you never *jump.* You're too scared."

His eyes narrowed. "You know what *I* don't want? To be someone's second choice. Or backup plan. I'm not the emotional security blanket you run to whenever the rest of your personal life doesn't work out."

They stood there, locked in a silence that crackled with frustration and something more complicated underneath—pain, confusion, longing.

"Well then," she said finally, voice cold, "I guess I'll see you after your date."

He nodded. "Yeah. And I guess I'll see you after *yours.*"

And just like that, they turned in opposite directions and walked away, the echo of their footsteps reverberating down the polished corridor, like the ending of a conversation that neither of them truly wanted to have.

Outside, the Swiss sun had begun its climb high above the distant mountains. The shadows stretched weirdly across the elegant stone walkways of the Syndicate's compound, mirroring the growing distance between two detectives who had once felt inseparable.

Dylan stepped out onto the street, her phone clutched tight in her hand. A message from Liam blinked on the screen: *Can't wait to see you. I'll be outside Café Vogel at 5. Just like old times.* She exhaled shakily.

Dillon, meanwhile, was already stepping into a sleek black vehicle, where Germandt sat in the front seat, smiling politely. "Ms. Vyra will be delighted."

Dillon leaned back in his seat, closed his eyes, and forced himself to forget everything that had just happened. But he couldn't. Suddenly, everything was wrong.

Chapter Twelve

The Follow

Vyra was dressed for casual time on a train. Her low-neck cashmere sweater, fashion jeans, and white sneakers only helped accentuate her almost girl-next-door beauty. "I'm so glad you agreed to accept my invitation." She reached back and took Dillon by the hand and guided him to his seat. She made a point of standing back up to put her purse on the rack above them. Her tiptoe stretch affected Dillon immediately.

To get to the truth, Dillon realized he would have to play it opposite of what she was expecting. "Does that move work on all your conquests?"

Without missing a beat, she said, "One hundred percent of the time." Vyra sat down and leaned forward. "Am I still batting a hundred?"

Dillon looked out the window. "Where are you taking me?"

"I have us returning to Zurich and then on to Lucerne. It's famous for its covered bridge, among other things. I've made a reservation for us on the upstairs balcony of a little restaurant close by. I picked a direct route, so the trip will be about two hours out and back. Well, that gives you enough time?'

"Enough time for what? To fall under your spell? To fall madly in love with you?"

Vyra sat back. "Germandt told me a little bit about your fight with Dylan. It reminds me of that song, how does it go, oh yes, 'Is she going to stay with the one who loves her or is she going back to the one she loves.' I always loved that turn of phrase."

Dillon protested immediately. "What? I don't love her. We're close partners, that's all."

"Alright, I see, but you should see your face right now." Vyra smiled. "Even I don't stand a chance, or do I? Do you need someone to get over her with?" Vyra laughed out loud.

“Believe me, you're not my type." Dillon’s face showed otherwise.

"Stop it. I'm everybody’s type. Anyway, at the very least, I'll be happy to take your mind off her. Consider it my gift to you." Vyra reached her hand out to touch his. "Oh, and I have an actual gift for you." She reached into her handbag and pulled out a small jewelry style box. "Open it!"

Dillon opened the box and found a man's watch inside. It was a replica of the Swiss train station clock visible on every train platform. The second hand clicked one second at a time, and he noticed the watch was perfectly in sync with the bigger clock outside the train car. All he felt comfortable saying was, “Thanks."

"I noticed you weren't wearing one. I hope you always think of me when you wear it." Vyra pretended to trace the watch on Dillon’s wrist.

After the touch, Dillon moved his hand back slowly. "You are alluring, I'll give you that.” He looked at the watch and then back into her eyes. “I can’t afford to get even a little lost in those eyes of yours.”

Vyra chuckled out loud. "Thank you for noticing my eyes. Anyway, you might not even care, you know, if you got temporarily lost.” Vyra decided not to push it too far for now. “Now, ask me your questions."

Dillon went back to look out the window at the scenery. "Would you mind if we just sat in silence for a while?"

Vyra turned to look out the window. "Sure, but just for a while." She chuckled, "A girl like me will want attention, and lots of it, later on."

The pair enjoyed looking at the endless farms that passed by the window. There were fields of sunflowers and fields of vegetables. There was a smattering of towns, with small businesses and houses surrounding the church steeples. The Swiss people walked, rode bicycles, and drove cars in an effort to accomplish the day's errands. Dillon wondered if he envied them just a little. But his mind's eye soon took him away from everyday life and into every passing background. There were the world-famous mountains. Tall and majestic. Radiant and picturesque.

Dillon took it all in and, at the same time, kept replaying his entire conversation with Dylan. Every time it replayed, he wished he had said something else, something wittier or more to the point.

Upon arriving in Lucerne, the couple whisked themselves off to a side street near the downtown bridge. The restaurant was empty except for them, and they took the table on the balcony overlooking the river. Swans were gliding effortlessly with the current as they inspected the people on the banks for bread. It was a blue-sky day, and the river was a blue-green color Dillon would commit to memory.

Just after lunch, Vyra stood and moved to the balcony railing, and Dillon followed. She pulled him close. "Enough of this silence. I've been wanting to try something all day." She planted one soft kiss on Dillon's lips and then followed with a longer-lasting one. "Did you enjoy that?"

Dillon nodded yes, but he lied. *She definitely knows how to give a kiss.* But something was off. There was no *real* meaning or intention, just technique. *I wonder what Dylan's kisses are like.*

"Never mind," Vyra stepped back, "That was my gift to you. Not the kiss, although, may I say, bravo. It was meant as a little test. I'm absolutely sure you weren't thinking about me as much as some other lucky girl."

She was right! "Thank you, I guess."

Vyra spoke calmly. "Don't look, but Germandt has been following us this whole time." Vyra returned to the table to collect her sweater and purse. "I should really be thanking you. I've been looking for the right moment to make him jealous. Maybe now he'll make a move and tell me how he feels. Maybe he'll even make an honest woman of me."

Dillon followed back to the return train. As the train pulled out, he said, "How long has Germandt been puppy dogging you?"

"Your assessment may not have been that flattering, but it's accurate enough." Vyra moved into a whisper. "It started just after I was married, and Germandt was promoted to Iglesia's inner circle. My husband never trusted him." Vyra reflected and was temporarily lost in thought. "Back then, I was even younger, immature, and married to an older man. I don't know why, but it felt good to have another younger man's eyes all over me. I guess you could call me an attention whore. Germandt and I had our moment, however so brief. A few months ago, I changed. Matured. I ended it quickly and quietly with Germandt. He didn't take it well at first, but then he realized his place."

Dillon looked down the train corridor and saw Germandt's face duck back. "He's still with us."

"Sure. Truth be told, I feel safe with him following me everywhere." Vyra and Dillon changed trains for their final twenty-minute leg back to Mannedorf. Germandt tried his best not to be seen by jumping into the passenger car toward the back of the train.

Vyra managed to touch Dillon's hand again. "Thank you. Truly. I've had such a good time. I'd forgotten how it felt to have a 'no strings attached' playdate."

Dillon grimaced. "I never asked you anything about the bombing."

Vyra stood up, turned, and beamed her brightest smile. "That was my plan. Oh, look, we've arrived."

Chapter Thirteen

Germandt

Germandt moved through the Syndicate's halls like a shadow, silent and measured. He'd memorized every twist and offshoot, every forgotten corridor and false turn. His eyes scanned each passage as he passed, always searching—though he already knew where his steps would take him.

They always led to her.

The security office suite welcomed him with a soft hum of machines and a low wash of blue light. It was his ritual. As always, he took a few moments to gaze up at the banks of surveillance monitors, watching the compound's life flicker across the screen—empty meeting rooms, sterile labs, coded doors. And then finally, movement: a glimpse of Vyra, slipping through the west corridor in a fitted white coat like some rare, uncatchable creature.

She was always a step ahead. He couldn't help but wonder if she *wanted* to be chased.

He used to think it was a coincidence, this constant game of hide and seek. But now? Now he suspected she did it on purpose. She was testing him. Training him, maybe. To chase. To crave. To need.

He rubbed his jaw, frustrated with himself. *You knew what you were getting into,* he reminded himself. *You told yourself you could handle her.* But that was just one of the many lies he now told himself daily. Lying to himself had become second nature—just another function of survival.

She had him twisted around her little finger from the moment they met.

He remembered that it had been just after her honeymoon with Iglesia. She was incandescent back then—sun-kissed skin, honey-glazed eyes, her laughter echoing like music down the halls. He remembered the moment he first saw her: descending the marble staircase like a goddess in human form, radiating confidence and control. He hadn't just fallen—he'd plummeted. Heart-first.

And somehow, impossibly, she noticed him too.

It started small. A brush of the arm. A subtle smile. The way she held his gaze a few seconds too long. She flirted with precision, like she was testing out the levers of a new machine—gauging his reactions, calibrating his attention. He knew exactly what she was doing. And he didn't care.

When Iglesia left on an extended business trip, she didn't wait long.

She invited him to her bedroom like it was the most natural thing in the world. No drama. No build-up. Just Vyra, in silk and moonlight, asking him with her eyes if he was ready to be owned. And he was. Entirely.

They spent a week tangled in luxury, in heat, in whispered promises he knew would dissolve the moment Iglesia returned.

And when the boss returned, Vyra didn't even flinch.

She made the boundaries clear. She was loyal. That week had been a fling. A spark in the dark. A necessary indulgence.

Germandt had smiled, nodded, and told her he understood.

But he didn't. His mind knew there was no way to avoid seeing her and to avoid wanting her.

That week hadn't just changed his life—it had *rewired* it. Every moment since then, his senses lived in that space. Her perfume. Her skin. The sound of her laughter from another room.

Once you've stood in the orbit of that kind of beauty, that kind of *power*, how could you ever go back to normal? He told himself he had to find a way to stay close. To *cement* himself to her, even if only as her guard, her shadow, her ever-loyal watcher.

And then, almost inevitably, the fantasy began: *What if Iglesia didn't come back next time? What if something happened to him? What if Vyra was finally free?*

The first time the thought passed through his mind, it felt alien. Wrong. Like something planted by someone else. And then he realized—it *had* been planted. By *her.*

With her tiny remarks. Her silence. Her careful framing of their time together as a secret tragedy. As something better left unspoken but never forgotten.

She knew how to manipulate. She had mastered it.

He never thought about what would happen if Iglesia found out about the affair. Or worse—what Iglesia would do to *Vyra*. On the rare occasion that thought crept in, he had to crush it. His mind wouldn't allow it to bloom.

But now Iglesia is dead. The threat was gone. And still, she kept him at arm's length.

What is she waiting for?

The questions haunted him, circling through his head in endless rotation: *Why hasn't she reached out again? Why no more nights? Why the distance?* She's back to being single now. The world had shifted. They could be something real.

And yet—nothing.

Sure, she gave him crumbs. The occasional smile, the occasional late-night conversation that hinted at something deeper. But she hadn't *invited* him again. She hadn't *chosen* him.

And that terrified him.

He followed her everywhere now. Told himself it was for her safety. That he was her protector. But he knew the truth—he was watching to make sure she didn't fall for someone else.

Someone like Dillon.

Dillon. The private detective. The American.

Germandt clenched his fists at the memory of that train ride to Lucerne. Dillon was calm, clever, and too casual. Vyra laughed at his jokes. Leaned in close. Her eyes lingered on him in ways Germandt recognized too well.

And then—*she kissed him. Twice!*

They were only playful, light, and meaningless kisses.

But not to Germandt. Not when it came from *her.*

That kiss burned in his brain like a brand. He couldn't sleep after that. Couldn't think clearly. The idea of Vyra choosing someone else, especially someone like *him,* was intolerable.

Right then and there, Germandt made a vow.

It didn't matter how foolish it sounded. *Dillon will not have her.* He would see to it. Personally.

He trailed them all the way back from Lucerne to the Syndicate's laboratory. Watched them part ways like old lovers pretending to be friends. He stood in the shadows and let the jealousy snake through him, tightening around his ribs until it almost suffocated him.

And then—clarity.

He laughed. A quiet, bitter laugh. What was he doing? Letting a woman twist him into knots? He wasn't built for this.

He wasn't going to let her humiliate him anymore.

The jealousy broke like a fever, and in its place, a cold resolve settled into his bones. No more waiting. No more hoping. No more chasing.

If Vyra didn't want him, fine.

He'd aim higher.

He'd go for the top.

Phase Two, he called it. A new plan. One that might require sacrifices—including her. But once he sat in the boss's chair, who would care?

Vyra had used her beauty to gain power. Germandt would make moves to grab his own power. And once he had that power, *he* would be the one to choose a partner, a life mate.

He told himself that. Over and over.

He was getting very good at rationalization.

Chapter Fourteen

The Truth About Exes

The next morning, Dylan walked into the conference room exuding confidence. She sat down, took out her cell, and started browsing. "I'd like to start going over the footage of the bombing one more time."

Dillon was hyperaware of the message his partner was sending. He took a deep and noticeable breath. "Did you and Liam reconnect in the way you wanted to?"

"We kissed."

"Oh."

"We kissed more than once."

"Please spare me the details." Dillon was sunk. *I can't believe this is happening. This came out of nowhere. And now I've lost any chance with her.*

It was easy for Dylan to read his face and his thoughts. "I don't mind telling you it was exciting at first. It was both familiar and new. I don't have to tell you it was validation. I was the one he should have been with, stayed with, and that felt great. I won. Do you know what I'm trying to describe to you?"

Dillon decided to be gracious. "Now that you're back with him, what does it mean for the detective agency, our partnership?"

"Well, hold on just a minute, I wasn't finished." Dylan used her hands to smooth out some wrinkles she detected on her pants. "While all this was going on. And all those old feelings came rushing back, I was also remembering all the bad. After all, what had I really won? Another chance with this guy. It felt like a reboot, and I could picture everybody, including myself, not liking it nearly as much as the first run."

Dillon perked up a little. "Is that so?"

"And then a funny thing happened. He didn't matter anymore. He just didn't." She paused. "I also heard your words ringing in my ears." Dylan looked down at her shoes. "Not only did I realize you were right, but it felt wrong to be kissing him when I was thinking about you." She waited for Dillon to understand the true meaning of that last line.

He got it right away. He stood up and crossed to her. "Please stand up."

"Why?"

"Just do it, OK."

Dylan stood up slowly, and on the way up, her mind began running. It was as if her brain had heard a starting gun.

Dillon leaned in and touched her lips with his. He drew back just for a second until her eyes opened, and then he gave her another kiss. Fireworks!

Dylan couldn't think through all the possibilities of what was happening, so she gave up and leaned into the moment. Fireworks!

He held her close and said, "I can't tell you how long I've wanted to do that." Dillon smiled. "Now I've won."

“Again. Kiss me again!” She suddenly realized all a kiss could be.

“Sure.” He waited for a beat after the kiss and then said, “How’s that?” Dillon was now holding her tightly around her waist.

She melted. This felt real. This felt safe, but in a good way. "Let's go on a real date when we get back to Daytona. Promise me."

"Sure. But before that happens, we have a case to solve." Dillon moved to separate.

Dylan took his hand. "One more thing. I know I sent mixed signals. First, I trash the idea of a slow romantic burn and then turn right around and hope Liam would sweep me off my feet."

"Really," Dillon chuckled, "I hadn't noticed."

"Well, I just wanted to tell you that, um, either style or some combination is fine by me. I want you and me to do this thing the way we feel. Does that make sense?"

"Yes, that makes perfect sense," Dillon was now grinning, "But you have a distinct advantage."

"How so?"

"You now know that I'm totally into you, and that gives you the edge."

Dylan smiled demurely. "I guess. But just so you know, I sent Liam packing. I guess that means you know you're the only one courting me."

"Advantage me." Dillon now leaned in for one more short kiss and then said, "Oh, and one more thing I think you should know...I mean, one more thing, I think we should talk about."

"Sounds serious."

Dillon motioned for them both to sit. "Do you remember me telling you about my ex-girlfriend, ah, finance, Saffron?"

"Why, did she just fly to Switzerland, too?"

"No, silly, she's happy somewhere else with someone else."

"I remember you were engaged after only a few months." Dylan checked her memories. "You said she got texts from her last boyfriend, and then she ended it and went back to...oh, now I get it."

Dillon looked deep into her eyes. "It wasn't all her fault. I worked too much." He swallowed hard. "The truth is, I just plain got bored. I can see that now and say it out loud. I wanted you to know the truth, because if in the next few months, you sometimes feel like I'm pulling away..."

Dylan was resolute. "Let's agree right here and now that we'll keep each other honest, and that we'll communicate like this when we feel something is wrong. Deal?"

"Deal." Dillon started immediately scripting ahead through the next months. He asked, "Maybe it's because we spent all this time together, you know, ever since the cruise ship heist, that I feel like this relationship is farther along than most new romances. One could even say that this upcoming date in Daytona is our fourth or fifth overall date. Maybe we should explore..."

"Stop right there. I'm expecting at least three real dates. Just us, and no work discussions."

Dillon sounded defeated. "Oh."

Dylan smiled and turned her chair to face her laptop. "Otherwise, what would we tell the kids?"

Dillon laughed.

She started to power up her laptop and then abruptly stopped. "Hey, you never told me any details about your 'date' with Vyra."

"Nothing to tell really. I was the patsy. The whole time she knew Germandt was following us, and she used me to make him jealous."

"Oh." Dylan felt somehow very relieved.

Dillon smirked. "Oh, and we kissed."

Silence.

Suddenly, Dylan's whole body lurched when she woke. Her head had been on the conference room table, and a small amount of drool was in front of her on her notepad. It took a minute for her to figure out she had been dreaming. The whole thing was one detailed movie-style dream. She shook off the cobwebs and steadied herself. She reached for a comb when Dillon walked in.

Dillon was all business. "I'd like us both to go over the footage of the bombing one more time." He looked at Dylan and tried to read her demeanor.

Dylan stared straight ahead.

Dillon asked, "Anything else I should know? Anything about yesterday?"

Dylan turned the laptop to face her, "No, nothing at all. And if you don't have anything to share, then let's get to it."

She launched herself back into the case, but in the back of her mind, she couldn't help but wonder what her dream really meant.

Chapter Fifteen

The Fire Door

An exasperated Dillon threw his pen down onto the conference table. "We've been going back over the same lab video footage for the last hour. I don't see anything new. Just the same steps, same hallway, same boom."

Dylan sighed and leaned closer to the monitor. "Let's agree to watch it one last time. Just once more, frame by frame."

She hit 'play.' The digital feed rolled forward in a clinical wash of grayscale. "Here's where we see Lutz and Iglesia walking down the hallway. They stop just in front of the big room with the large machine. Iglesia starts moving toward the door. Then Lutz runs up to him and—boom. There's our explosion. Right there."

She froze the frame, tapping at the timestamp.

Dillon squinted. "Wait! That timestamp skips a half-second."

"Yeah," Dylan agreed, rubbing her eyes. "Which means we lost something. That millisecond could've shown us everything. Maybe even how the bomb was detonated or who was closest."

Dillon leaned back in his chair and stared at the ceiling. "The timeline feels critical. But we've both watched every second of this, over and over. I guess that's all we've got."

Dylan wasn't ready to give up. "We're missing something. I know it. We need to think outside the box."

"Clues. We're missing clues," Dillon echoed, eyes now closed. "Okay, detective's rulebook. What does 'Detective 101' say when you're stuck?"

Dylan smiled wistfully. "Wow. I was just about to call Dad. He'd know what to do."

"You know," Dillon said gently, "that's normal after someone passes. You still try to reach for them. But those memories—you carry those. You'll always have your favorite times to relive. Not a day goes by that I don't think about my..."

Dylan suddenly bolted upright, eyes alight. "That's it!"

Dillon blinked. "What's it?"

"You were talking, and certain words just *popped*. 'Adjust,' 'not being there,' 'earlier'. It hit me. Earlier! Earlier in the day!" She was already halfway down the hallway. "I'll be right back!"

Within minutes, she returned with the compound's security officer in tow—a stocky man with a utility belt and a no-nonsense face.

"Can we see the footage earlier in the morning? The day of the explosion. You know, the very first thing in the morning when everyone is reporting for work?" Dylan asked, barely catching her breath.

The officer nodded. "Should be able to queue it up on the back wall display." He moved to the mounted television, fiddling with a keypad and remote. "I'll send the feed from our archives. You'll be able to pause and make your way through using this." He handed Dylan the remote.

The screen flickered, then filled with clear footage marked 8:00 AM.

The lab was quiet at first. Then the usual trickle of white-coated technicians began to appear, checking in, powering on terminals, adjusting equipment.

"There!" Dylan shouted, lunging forward to pause the feed. She pointed at the lower part of the screen. "Isn't that Vyra and Germandt entering the lab?"

Dillon leaned in. "Yup. That's them. Let's see where it goes."

Dylan pressed play. Germandt opened the door for another man. He was dressed in janitorial garb, a baseball cap pulled low over his eyes. Suspiciously ordinary.

The detectives watched the footage as Vyra and Germandt continued into the hallway, paused for a moment near a corner, then turned and left the way they came. The janitor followed—pausing at the same spot, then exiting behind them without ever logging an entry.

Dylan's voice was low, grim. "There's our bomber. Slipped in behind them, no sign-in, no identity verification. He just... walked in."

Dillon rubbed his jaw. "The real question is—did Vyra and Germandt *accidentally* let him in? Or did they do it *on purpose*?"

"My money's on *purpose*," Dillon said darkly.

The video continued to play. A moment later, something caught Dillon's eye.

"Pause it right there."

The screen froze on a lab room tucked toward the corner. It was noticeably empty.

"That room," Dillon said, pointing. "All the other labs have people working. Why's this one empty?"

"Could be anything," Dylan replied. "Tech might've called in sick. Or maybe that room's for storage?"

Dillon didn't respond. He was now pointing at another corner of the screen.

"There. That last technician walking in… and someone's with him."

The display showed what appeared to be a lab tech and a younger man entering the facility and heading straight for the empty lab. Dylan paused the tape and stepped out into the hallway, calling back the security officer.

He returned quickly, slightly out of breath. "What's up?"

"Can you ID this technician?"

He leaned closer. "Yeah, that's Gilbear."

"And the man with him?"

The officer nodded slowly. "That's his younger brother. He's on the spectrum. Autistic. Gilbear sometimes has to bring him in when he doesn't have anyone to watch him at home."

"Can you confirm the brother isn't the bomber?"

"Absolutely. We ruled him out on day one. Completely innocent. Just an unlucky kid who happened to be in the wrong place at the worst time." With that, the officer left.

Dylan turned to Dillon with a gleam in her eyes. "We've been counting the casualties wrong."

"What do you mean?"

"Think about it. The official body count is fourteen. But we now know Gilbear's brother was inside. That makes *fifteen*. Unless—"

"—someone got out," Dillon finished, eyes narrowing.

"Exactly." Dylan fast-forwarded the footage to the moment of the explosion. “Watch closely. I’ll try to pause it one second before the blast.”

It took her three tries, but she caught a single blurry frame right before detonation.

"There. Look at this."

The frame showed Lutz absorbing the brunt of the blast. His body was mid-air, already flung forward into Iglesia. Then the frame showed the bodies meeting and Iglesia being hurled into the panic bar of the fire exit door. On the edge of the screen, where the door met the wall, a thin shaft of light—daylight—was visible.

Dillon sat forward. "That sliver of light... the door opened."

Dylan nodded. "The force of the blast may have thrown Iglesia straight through. And that door leads to the emergency stairwell that exits below the lab."

They turned to each other, silent, and at the same time began to speak—

"Iglesia is..."

They caught themselves mid-sentence and glanced up at the conference room’s camera.

Their eyes locked. Without speaking, they mouthed the same phrase: *Alive!* Both detectives were thinking the same thing. *You know who may still be alive.*

Dylan was already halfway to the door when Dillon caught her by the arm and spun her gently around.

"I know what you’re thinking. I know exactly what you’re about to do." His voice was low and serious. "But I say... we hold this close. Keep it quiet for now."

Dylan looked like she wanted to argue, but instead, she nodded once, solemnly.

They both returned to the table and pretended to rewatch the footage for the benefit of the surveillance. They exchanged no words, just the occasional sigh or click of the remote. But their hands were now texting under the table, furiously exchanging theories, implications, and next steps.

As the footage reached its end, another detail caught their attention. In one of the final frames, just as the chaos erupted, there was a flicker of light below the lab floor. A stairwell light, or maybe something else.

"Someone exited the back," Dylan whispered.

"And if that someone *was* Iglesia," Dillon said quietly, "then everything changes."

They sat in silence for a moment, the gravity of their discovery settling around them like a storm cloud.

A bomb had gone off. People had died. But the man everyone thought was dead may have slipped through the fire door and vanished into the daylight—setting into motion something far larger than either detective had imagined.

And they were now the only two who knew.

For now.

Chapter Sixteen

Tripwire

The hallway was quiet, humming with the low murmur of voices and the occasional echo of footsteps. Fluorescent lights flickered above, casting a sterile blue-white tone over the corridor. Just around the bend, Vyra and Germandt were locked in a hushed conversation. Germandt frowned sharply, muttered something, and stormed off, his footsteps fading quickly as he turned the corner.

Vyra turned, saw Dillon, and raised a hand to beckon him over. Her face bore a faint smile—strained, perhaps, but trying to stay cordial.

"This will just take a second," Dillon murmured to Dylan, nodding toward Vyra. He stepped forward but stopped cold mid-stride.

Just beyond Vyra, a janitor pushed a metal cart slowly down the corridor. He wore navy coveralls and a familiar baseball cap, tugged low. Dillon's eyes narrowed. Something wasn't right. Every instinct screamed at him, and the hair on his arms and neck stood on end.

Something subtle—offbeat in the rhythm of the hallway.

Dillon's eyes flicked downward. The carpet was a dull gray with a faint geometric pattern, but something caught the light on the floor level. A nearly invisible thread stretched tightly across the floor—anchored to a bolt screw on the wall, running across the hallway toward the glass balcony railing.

It pressed against his right pant leg.

"Dylan," he called behind him, voice firm, "Don't move. Tripwire. Stay exactly where you are."

Dylan froze, midway through stepping forward. "What?"

He pointed down, slowly. "Tripwire. I mean it. Don't take another step."

She crouched to see. The bright morning sun filtered through the high windows and caught a glint of tensioned wire. There it was—a sliver of reflection and the faintest shadow cast on the floor. Her breath caught in her throat.

"I see it," she whispered. "I think I can get to it."

"No." Dillon's voice was sharp, desperate. "Please go back. Please. A thousand things can go wrong—even if you don't touch the wire."

But Dylan wasn't listening. She moved with slow, deliberate control. Crouching beside Dillon, she studied the wire, then his pant leg.

"Relax your leg," she instructed calmly. "Let it fall back naturally. Don't tense up."

Her hands gently pulled at the fabric, guiding it back away from the wire. With one smooth motion, the pant leg retreated from danger. As soon as he was free, Dillon grabbed Dylan by the arm and yanked her to her feet.

"Run!" he yelled.

The two detectives sprinted down the hallway in the opposite direction, hearts hammering, diving to the ground just as they heard the sound of a sharp movement behind them.

Back at the scene, the janitor with the baseball cap had been watching carefully. His eyes locked on the wire. He reached into his pocket and pulled out a small, battered metal box with a prominent red button on top. He was just about to press it when Vyra—reacting faster than anyone expected—rushed him from the side. With a sudden grunt, she body-checked him, sending the box flying.

Both detectives, lying on the ground, turned in time to see it.

The moment froze.

It was like a movie frame suspended in time—every detail crystal clear. The janitor's eyes widened with panic. Vyra fell sideways mid-collision. The trigger box flipped in mid-air, catching the sunlight as it twisted. For Dylan, the world seemed to pause, the air itself vibrating with tension.

Her mind shot backward to just half an hour before. She had been *bursting* to tell someone—Iglesia was alive. The video footage showed him, alive and possibly escaping through the fire door just a split second before the lab explosion. But Dillon had made her wait. He insisted they keep the discovery close to the chest—for now.

They had spent the last thirty minutes furiously texting, crafting a plan to gather the regional directors and Mr. Haus in one room. "We need to control the narrative," Dillon had said. "If we spook the wrong person, they'll vanish—or worse, strike again."

Questions had swirled in Dylan's head ever since. Did Vyra know? Did Germandt? Were they collaborators or pawns? How deeply did this conspiracy run? And if Iglesia was still alive—where was he now?

She snapped back to the present. The trigger box clattered to the ground. It tumbled, bounced, skidded—and landed. The red button stayed mercifully untouched. Silence followed.

Everyone stared, unmoving.

Dylan's breath returned in a shallow, gasping rush. Vyra groaned and pushed herself up on one elbow, shaken but unhurt. Dillon stood slowly, scanning the hallway, eyes narrowed.

Then—movement.

The janitor was up, bolting down the corridor toward the emergency stairwell. He didn't look back.

"I'm going after him!" Dillon shouted.

Before Dylan could argue, he was already gone—bounding down the hallway, leaping over the side rail of the stairwell like a hurdler clearing a fence, and vanishing through the lower door.

Dylan turned her attention to Vyra. "Are you hurt?"

Vyra shook her head, brushing her hair back. "No. Just stunned."

"You saved our lives."

Vyra didn't answer immediately. She looked toward the trigger box, still lying inert on the carpet.

"I think I saw him before," she said, her voice tight. "I wasn't sure. I didn't want to sound paranoid. But when I saw his hand reach for something—I didn't think, I just reacted."

Dylan nodded. "You did well."

She reached down, gently plucked the box from the floor with the tips of her fingers, and placed it inside a clear evidence bag she had retrieved from her satchel. Carefully, she turned back to the tripwire and traced it to its mount. It had been expertly strung—

too well for a spontaneous job. The rigging was sophisticated, precise.

This had been premeditated. Set in place and left to catch a target.

She looked at Vyra again, studying her. “You’re sure you didn’t know who that man was?”

Vyra met her eyes. “I swear. I didn’t recognize him—not until I saw what he was trying to do.”

Dylan believed her—for now. “Listen, warn everyone about that tripwire until it’s been disabled.”

She pulled out her phone and checked her partner's locator. He was on foot nearby.

She turned to one of the guards who had come running at the sound of commotion.

“Lock down all stairwells,” Dylan instructed. “Nobody leaves or enters without ID and clearance from me or Dillon.”

“Yes, ma’am.”

She stepped aside, her mind racing again. **Was this tripwire meant for her? Dillon? Or someone else?** The placement... the timing... it didn’t feel random. It felt like a message.

She looked back down the hall. People were starting to emerge again. A few security guards stood talking in hushed tones. ‘Wet floor’ signs were stationed on all sides of the tripwire.

Dylan knew the clock was ticking. Whoever had orchestrated the lab bombing was still playing their game—and the players were growing bolder. First, a bomb. Now a tripwire, in plain sight.

Dylan knew one thing: the pressure was closing in on someone. And pressure had a way of forcing mistakes.

She only hoped the next mistake wouldn't cost them more lives.

Dillon returned a few minutes later, breathing heavily, a streak of sweat cutting through the dust on his face.

"He was ready," he said grimly. "Knew the layout. Knew the exits. There's no way he came in through official means."

Dylan held up the clear bag with the trigger box inside. "We'll need this analyzed immediately. Maybe prints. Maybe something else."

"And the tripwire?" Dillon asked.

"Professional grade. Not some DIY job," she answered. "This wasn't meant to scare us. It was meant to kill."

They stared down the hallway where it had all happened—just another corridor in a pristine facility, but now it felt like a minefield.

Dillon finally said, "We need to call that meeting. All of them. Haus, directors, Vyra, Germandt."

"And when we do," Dylan added, eyes hardening, "we drop the truth on them all at once."

They stood shoulder to shoulder, the weight of the moment pressing on both their backs. They looked out the window in hopes that the lake in front of them might steady their resolve.

Just then, Dillon saw the janitor climb out of a waste bin near the loading dock. He casually tossed his ball cap in the trash and started filing in behind the exiting workers.

"There he is!" Dillon was off in a flash, running again, and with renewed purpose.

Chapter Seventeen

The Bomber

Dillon raced around the side of the building, his shoes hammering the pavement, each step echoing through the narrow alley. The early morning sun cast sharp angles of shadow between the service entrance and the loading dock. He spotted the janitor again—no, the bomber—just as the man tried to duck between a dumpster and the concrete wall. Dillon surged forward, cutting him off.

"Hey!" Dillon shouted.

The man skidded to a halt, turned, and ripped off his ball cap. His hands trembled as he unzipped the front of his coveralls. Beneath, he wore a bomb vest strapped tight to his chest. Blocks of explosives were woven into the fabric, wires threaded in and out like some horrific quilt. A trigger box dangled from his hand—one twitch, and that was it.

"Don't come any closer!" he barked. "I mean it! I'll touch this thing off!"

Dillon stopped dead, holding both palms in the air. The air between them felt electric with panic.

"You don't have to do that," Dillon said calmly. "Look at me—I'm not moving. I'm not going to come near you unless you say it's okay."

A beat of silence passed. The bomber's chest rose and fell rapidly. Sweat beaded along his forehead. Dillon's eyes flicked between the trigger, the vest, and the man's unstable breathing.

Just then, Dylan turned the corner, boots crunching on gravel. She came around casually, not expecting anything out of the ordinary. But the second she laid eyes on the bomber, she froze mid-step. Her hand instinctively moved to her hip, where her sidearm rested.

She backed behind the corner of the building and took cover behind a steel post. Slowly, she peeked out to assess the situation. Dillon was too close. If the man detonated, he'd be caught in the blast radius. Maybe worse.

She called out, projecting her voice clearly. "Dillon. It's me. I'm behind the building, about twenty feet from you. I've got cover."

Dillon didn't take his eyes off the man. His jaw clenched, but he smiled faintly. "I'm glad to hear your voice."

"Who's that?!" the man shouted, eyes darting around. His grip on the trigger box tightened. The veins in his neck bulged.

"That's just my partner," Dillon said quickly. "She won't come any closer. I promise. We're not here to hurt you."

He kept his voice low and even. His instincts screamed at him to do something, anything—but what? One wrong move could kill them all. He took a careful breath.

"What's your name?" Dillon asked.

The bomber didn't answer. His eyes were wild now, darting left, then right, then to the ground. Dillon tried another tactic.

"Look, we don't care about you—honestly. We were hired to find the bomber. That's it. We get paid if we find the bomber. If we blow up here, I don't get a check, and neither do you."

A flicker of confusion crossed the man's face. He shifted uncomfortably, and Dillon saw the wires tremble slightly. Too close. Way too close.

"I don't think you acted alone," Dillon continued, softening his tone. "Someone hired you. I think you're working for someone way above your pay grade."

"I'm not telling you anything," the man snapped. "Not a damn thing."

Dillon saw it now—panic, yes, but also guilt. Regret. His grip on the box was tighter now, as if the only thing keeping him grounded was the ability to end it all. His hand shook.

"Then don't *say* anything," Dillon suggested. "Let's play a game. I'll say some names, and you don't have to talk. Just blink. Or maybe scratch your head, or—I don't know—wiggle your ear."

The bomber looked at him like he was crazy.

"I'm serious," Dillon said. "Then we'll know who's pulling your strings. We won't even care about you anymore."

Dillon took a breath and started. "Mr. Haus."

No reaction.

"Mr. Bank."

Still nothing.

"Ms. School? Mr. Museum? Vyra?"

Still stone-faced.

"Germandt?"

There it was. Subtle. A quick motion to wipe the sweat off his brow. A hard swallow. Dillon caught it.

The detective nodded slowly. “I thought so.”

The bomber’s eyes flared. “You don’t know what they’ll do to me. The Syndicate… they’ll kill me in an instant.”

Dillon stepped a half-inch closer—just enough to show solidarity, not threat. “What if I said I can protect you?”

The man laughed—bitter and broken. “How?”

Dillon faltered. He hadn’t thought that far ahead. “Well… I’m not sure, exactly. But I know people. We can put you somewhere. Get you a new life.”

The bomber’s expression collapsed. "No. It's over for me. I always knew I'd go out like this. Looking back, I don’t even know why I took this job… I guess I was tired of being invisible. Cleaning floors, fixing toilets, and eating lunch in janitor closets. And one day, someone notices me. Offers me a job that actually *matters*… and I said yes.”

Dillon tried to reach him. “You *do* matter. We’re talking right now. That’s something. You’ve still got a choice.”

“No,” the man said quietly. “Not anymore.”

He began scanning the area frantically. Left. Right. Behind. Looking for threats, for snipers, for the inevitable. Dillon knew it—the man was seconds away from pushing the button.

He tried one last time. “If you keep acting jumpy, my partner’s going to take a shot. She won’t miss.”

Dylan was already lining up her sight, listening to every word. Her breath was shallow, her arms steady. Dillon’s voice came through like a lifeline, but it was his code phrase that clicked.

“Hey, partner,” Dylan called out. “Remember our first case? When that woman shot her dad in the chest?”

Dillon didn’t miss a beat. “No, I think I remember her shooting him in the *hand*.”

Dylan smiled grimly. That was it. The signal.

The bomber looked confused. “Hey… what’s happening?”

Dylan leveled her sights. Steady. Exhale. “On your left!”

She fired.

The bullet sliced through the air and slammed into the bomber’s hand. Blood spurted, and he screamed, dropping the box—but it didn’t fall far. His left hand immediately caught it again, fumbling, shaking—

Dillon lunged forward. “No!”

Too late.

The man winced and slammed his thumb onto the button.

The explosion erupted with a dull roar, flames and smoke rising in a violent burst. Dylan felt the shockwave before she heard it, pushing her back behind the wall. Her ears rang. Her skin burned. She felt the heat scald her cheek.

She forced herself up, coughing, and ran toward the blast.

The scene was pure chaos. A small crater smoldered where the bomber had stood. Bits of concrete and metal littered the alley. Most of the blast had gone upward—but that wasn’t enough to spare anyone nearby.

“Dillon!” she screamed.

She spotted him—about fifteen feet away, crumpled beside a steel door. He’d been thrown like a rag doll, landing hard.

"Dillon, no—no, no, no!"

She sprinted to his side. His eyes were open but glazed with pain. His mouth moved, trying to say something.

"Don't move," she said quickly. "Stay still. You're going to be okay. I've got you."

She dropped to her knees, and her hands brushed something jagged sticking out of his side. Rebar. Shrapnel. Something unknown. Blood pooled under him. His leg, too—torn and raw.

"Don't talk," she said gently. "Just stay with me."

But he gave her a weak smile. "Great shot."

Tears broke from her eyes. "Shut up, you idiot."

She looked around, heart pounding. People were beginning to come out of the building. She looked back down at him, squeezing his hand.

"You're not going anywhere, okay? Not after all this."

He blinked slowly. "We got the bomber?"

"Yeah," she said, nodding. "We got him. Now stay with me."

Dillon was fading.

"I'm calling for help," she said, voice shaking. She yanked out her phone and dialed 1-1-2.

Chapter Eighteen

1-1-2!

The dispatcher spoke in clipped, precise German, the words coming fast but clear through Dylan's phone speaker.

"**1-1-2 operator. Was ist Ihr Notfall?**"

Dylan clenched her jaw, trying to keep breathing even. Her voice wavered at first, but she pressed it down with training and sheer force of will.

"I need an ambulance sent to my location. My partner—" she glanced down at Dillon's blood-covered body, "—was hit by shrapnel from a bomb. We're at the corner of Main and Mettlenstrasse. Up by the old convent. Please hurry!"

She could feel Dillon's blood soaking into the knees of her skirt. The metallic tang filled her nostrils, clinging to the back of her throat. His face was pale. Too pale. He was conscious but fading fast.

The dispatcher shifted to English instantly. "Hold one."

Hold one? What? Dylan stared at her phone like it had betrayed her.

Hold what? Time? Breath? My sanity? she thought, fighting the urge to scream. *He's dying in my arms, and you're asking me to hold one?*

She almost demanded a supervisor when the voice returned, sharper now, more focused.

"I have an ambulance dispatched. ETA three minutes. I am connecting you now with Dr. Gupta from the University Hospital Emergency Trauma. Go ahead, Dr. Gupta."

The voice that followed was calm, unwavering, and oddly comforting. A soft British accent came through. "Hello, this is Dr. Gupta. Tell me quickly—what are the visible injuries? Focus on what is bleeding."

Dylan did a quick scan of Dillon's body, trying to keep her hands from trembling too much. "Two large bone fragments—human—one lodged in his lower abdomen, one in his right thigh. Both are bleeding steadily."

"Copy that," Gupta replied instantly. "I want you to remove the fragment from his leg. Now."

"What?!"

"Do it," he repeated. "Then insert your finger into the wound and press it up toward the femur. You're looking to clamp the femoral artery with pressure. If he bleeds out there, he's gone before the ambulance gets to you."

Dillon groaned loudly. His hand flopped to his side as Dylan hesitated.

"Do it now," Gupta snapped.

Gritting her teeth, Dylan reached for the protruding fragment in Dillon's thigh. Her fingers slipped the first time—blood made everything slick. Dillon let out a strangled cry as she pulled the bone loose, then shoved her finger into the wound.

It was like plunging her finger into a soaked sponge.

"Now find the artery. Press hard up toward the bone. Do you feel it? A pulsing thread?"

Dylan moved her fingertip, trying not to vomit. Then—there.

“Yes. Got it.”

“Good. Hold that pressure. Do not move your hand. Now switch your phone to speaker and find something long, preferably a cloth. A sock, a sleeve. You need to pack the abdominal wound, fast.”

Dylan fumbled to press the ‘speaker’ icon. The phone clattered to the ground next to Dillon’s head. She glanced down at her own clothes. Her skirt was long enough. She tore a large piece off with one hard rip, her hands shaking like leaves in a storm.

"Still holding?" Gupta asked.

"Yes."

"Now pack the cloth into the belly wound. Press it in firmly, but don’t dislodge the bone fragment.”

Her hands moved on autopilot, pushing fabric into the gory hole in Dillon’s abdomen. He let out a sound between a groan and a scream, his body arching, but he didn’t fight her.

“Breathe, Dillon,” she whispered. “Don’t you leave me. Breathe.”

His face was ghostly gray. Blood dribbled from the corner of his mouth. Dylan tried not to panic. His body trembled under her touch. Her own heart thundered in her chest like it wanted to burst out.

"How's his breathing?" Gupta's voice cut through the chaos again. “Ambulance should be pulling up any second.”

“He’s—he’s struggling. Chest is moving, but shallow. Skin is clammy.”

Dillon opened his eyes, just barely. “Tell him...” he rasped. “Tell him I’m breathing okay for a guy who just got blown up.”

A weak chuckle escaped his lips, and then he winced so hard his whole body spasmed. Dylan could see the pain tearing through him like an earthquake.

"I think I'm busted up pretty bad..." he murmured.

"I know, D," she whispered, brushing back his sweat-soaked hair. "But you're going to make it."

Then his eyes rolled back.

"Doc—he's crashing!"

She cried out, "No, no, no, stay with me! Dillon! Stay awake!"

The rising wail of a siren shattered the morning air like a promise. Dylan looked up as an ambulance screeched to a stop at the edge of the alley. Two EMTs burst out, wheeling a gurney, medical bags bouncing against their hips.

One of them knelt beside her instantly. "We've got him. Don't move your hand until I say."

"I've got the artery clamped," Dylan told them breathlessly. "Femoral. He was bleeding heavily."

"You saved his life," the EMT said without looking up, already snapping on gloves and barking orders to his partner in rapid German.

The second medic joined them and began unpacking trauma tools. A neck brace slipped around Dillon's head, monitors were attached to his chest, and a saline IV was jabbed into his arm. One EMT took over compressing the abdominal wound. Another lifted Dylan's hand and replaced it with a trauma clamp.

"You're done," the first EMT told her. "Step back."

Dylan stumbled to her feet, covered in blood from her elbows to her thighs. She watched as they loaded Dillon onto the stretcher. He groaned again—good, he was still alive. That sound, that small noise of pain, was the most beautiful thing she'd ever heard.

They pushed him into the ambulance, one of the medics riding in the back. Dylan didn't ask permission. She climbed in behind them, not even glancing at the bystanders beginning to gather down the block.

The doors slammed shut, and the siren wailed again.

The vehicle lurched forward.

Dillon's head rolled slightly toward her. His eyes fluttered open. He gave a weak smirk and then passed out again.

Dylan didn't take her eyes off him. Not for one second.

As they careened down Mettlenstrasse toward the hospital, she reached over and gently squeezed his hand.

"You're not dying on me, Dillon," she said softly. "We've still got a job to do."

She looked down at her partner, then back at the medic, who was checking vitals.

"He's stable," the medic nodded. "For now."

Dylan closed her eyes and let out a breath she hadn't realized she'd been holding.

She leaned her head back against the wall of the ambulance, and for the first time since the explosion, she let herself feel something other than fear.

Relief.

But it wouldn't last long.

She knew this wasn't over. Germandt was still out there. And someone had just tried to kill them both.

This case had just become very personal.

Chapter Nineteen

The Solve

Dylan hadn't left her partner's side. She sat slumped forward in a plastic chair that creaked every time she shifted her weight, chin resting near Dillon's arm. The hospital room was hushed except for the rhythmic beeping of machines and the hiss of an oxygen valve releasing in measured bursts. Outside the window, the Zurich skyline gleamed under a pale sun—but in here, time had stilled.

She was caught between a dream and a memory when Dillon stirred. A soft rustle of sheets and then—**beep, beep, beep.** The monitor let out a few high-pitched chimes. She jolted upright.

Her heart pounded. Every second since the bombing replayed itself in her mind like a cruel, broken film reel.

Why did he run after the janitor? Why didn't he see that stupidity? Why did he press the bomber? Why didn't my shot take him down in time? Why didn't I...

The loop tortured her. Even now, she kept mentally aiming again, re-firing, hoping her imaginary bullet might do better than the real one had.

Her hands folded together instinctively, fingers locking tight. Trouble never shook her faith, only sharpened it. She leaned forward, head almost resting on the bed rail, and quietly began to pray.

"*No harm shall overtake you,*" she whispered, "*no disaster will come near your tent. For He will command His angels concerning you, to guard you in all your ways...*"

There was a beat of silence.

Then a raspy voice. "Dylan? Are you praying over me? Is it that bad? How long do I have?"

Her eyes flew open. Dillon's voice—weak, dry, but unmistakably him.

She jumped to her feet, a sob halfway caught in her throat.

"Oh, you big faker! How long have you been awake?"

"Just long enough to make my peace," he croaked.

"Well, you're going to be around for way longer than that'll take." She laughed through the tears, the tension crumbling in her chest. Her voice cracked. "I was so worried. You don't even know..."

Dillon reached out and gently took her hand in his. His grip was light, but steady. "It'd be hard for you to train a new partner," he murmured. "And I didn't want to leave you like that." A faint smirk tugged at his lips. "Besides, I feel like we've got a lot more time together."

She smiled, wiping her eyes with her free hand. "Your stomach wound closed up clean, and the leg, too. You were in surgery for three hours. Doctor says you're lucky."

"Did you stay here the whole time?"

"I did."

"You didn't even leave to eat?" he asked, incredulous.

Dylan raised an eyebrow. "Swiss hospital food? I'm fasting for your soul."

He chuckled. "Don't you—we—have a case to solve?"

She stood, stretching. "They're releasing you in a couple of days. You know, Swiss doctors." She cleared her throat and put on a thick accent. "*Mein Junge, you must breathe the fresh air! Frische Luft ist gesund!*"

Dillon smirked. "Wow. You're really picking up Swiss German. It suits you."

He slowly pushed himself up on the bed. "Help me raise the back of this thing?"

Dylan found the control and clicked it upward until he was nearly seated.

"You're not going to believe the dream I had after surgery," he said, eyes wide. "It was like I was walking through the whole case in reverse. And it all started with the assumption that Iglesia is still alive."

She raised her eyebrows. "So, what's your dream solve?"

"Okay," he said, glancing down at the IV lines tangled at his wrists. "Follow me. Interrupt if you think I'm way off base. So—Vyra did it. Or at least she orchestrated it. Germandt was in love with her, or close to it. She dangled herself in front of him like a prize. Made him think her husband was the only thing standing between them."

Dylan's mouth twitched. "You think Vyra and Germandt planted the bomb?"

"No. I think Vyra *planted the idea*. I think she said, 'If only someone would get rid of my husband…' and Germandt, being an idiot in love, ran with it. He knew Iglesia's schedule. Probably got someone to plant the device—someone expendable, someone serial. He and Vyra keep their hands clean."

He paused, nodding toward the water cup on the tray. Dylan handed it to him and held the straw.

"Thanks. Anyway," he continued, "they had airtight alibis. Looked innocent. Vyra even flirted with me to throw me off."

Dylan crossed her arms. "You think she was using you?"

"C'mon, Dylan. You know I'm damaged goods in the romance department. She saw that. She used it. Played it up."

Dylan rolled her eyes but didn't argue.

Dillon said, "She got Germandt to do the dirty work, rewarded him for a job well done, and got her freedom and maybe a big payout to boot."

Dylan moved to the window, staring out at the clouds. Her eyes narrowed. "I'm with you... mostly," She said slowly. "But what was Vyra's endgame? If she just wanted Iglesia gone, she could've done it ten different ways. Why a bombing? Why all the layers?"

Dillon continued. "Remember when Mr. Haus told us no one knew what happened in that lab? And Vyra said her best guess was they were 'synthesizing a better drug'? What if Iglesia wasn't the target at all?"

Dylan blinked. "Go on."

"What if the *lab* was the target? And Iglesia getting blown up was just a... happy coincidence?"

She stared at him for a long beat. Then nodded. "That would throw us off. Make us chase a fake motive."

Dylan grabbed her phone, and her fingers quickly danced over the screen. "I'm going to look up Mr. Lutz. Let's see what he was working on."

A few seconds of silence as she scrolled. She found the obituary.

"He's survived by a wife of twenty years... holds multiple degrees in biology... and... there it is." She tapped the screen. "He specialized in genetic engineering. Gene patching. Some minor breakthroughs."

She hit the call button for the phone number attached to the article. "Voicemail. Erm—hi, this is the detective assigned to your husband's case. I have a few questions regarding any patents he may have held. Please call me back..."

Immediately after she hung up, a voice crackled on the line.

"Hallo?"

"Oh—hi! Mrs. Lutz?"

"Yes. What did you want to know? About my husband's patents?"

"Yes, please. Did he have any on file?"

"He did," the woman replied, her voice soft but tinged with weariness. "Several. Mostly for gene patching."

Dylan mouthed *yes*. "Do you happen to know the specific application?"

A long pause. "Not really. I wasn't a scientist, you know. But I believe one of them had something to do with—hmm—hair loss."

Dylan's face fell. "Not obesity?"

"No. Definitely not that."

Another pause. Then the woman said something that made Dylan bolt upright.

"But I don't have the patents anymore. A woman came to me right after the bombing. Very elegant. Said she was representing a pharmaceutical firm. Offered me two million euros to sign over the rights. I… I took the deal."

Dylan's eyes widened. "You signed them away?"

"I did. I just lost my husband. It felt like the right thing. I didn't know who else to trust."

"Do you remember the woman's name?"

"No. But she was…very confident. Maybe thirty-five."

Dylan thanked her and hung up. She stared at the phone in her hand for a long second, then slowly turned to Dillon.

"The bomb was meant for Lutz. I'm guessing the gene-patching patent is worth billions, especially for reversing hair loss. Vyra didn't want Iglesia dead. Not really. She wanted that *research*. The bombing was supposed to be a smokescreen."

Dillon sat back, eyes wide. "That explains everything. The lab. The misdirection. That's why Vyra was so willing to give up being a Syndicate director because she owned the patents."

Dylan grabbed her jacket. "This changes everything."

As she reached the door, Dillon called after her. "Hey."

She stopped. "Yeah?"

"You saved my life. In the alley. Don't think I'll forget that."

Dylan smiled faintly. "Good. Because I might need you to save mine next time."

She slipped into the hallway.

Meanwhile, in a different district of Zurich—far removed from the sterile white walls of the hospital—a man leaned back in a leather chair in a soundproof room.

He pulled a small earpiece from his ear and placed it into a velvet-lined case. The receiver beside him blinked off.

The walls around him were covered in soundboards, monitors, and frequencies, all silent now.

He poured a dark scotch and sipped it slowly.

Much had just been revealed.

Much was now known.

And now... now, it was his move.

This had been a very interesting day. A very interesting day indeed.

Chapter Twenty

One Valuable Pig

Dylan reread the seemingly random note she found near her bag. It simply read, 'Meet me in the basement fitness center at 10 am.' She told a still recuperating Dillon about it, and of course, he tried to talk her out of it. She had decided to go anyway.

She waited in silence until the large entryway door opened. Shadows of figures appeared and moved closer.

It was Vyra. She was in a wheelchair. She was being pushed by a very large and muscular young man. When the duo came to a stop, Dylan saw that Vyra's wrists were loosely zip-tied to her armrests. It was clear that she was experiencing the effects of a small amount of sedative. The man came around to the front, set the brakes, and then receded into a dark corner.

Dylan started to take a step forward. She stopped mid-step and decided to settle in. She couldn't help but wonder out loud, "What's happening now?"

"My friend," shouted an advancing figure, "How nice it is to see you alive and well again!" The man stepped into the light. It was him, average build and average looks, with a noticeably receding hairline as the only distinguishing trait. Dylan recognized him from the dossier and the surveillance videos. This man had a few newer-looking burn marks and scars, but it certainly was Iglesia.

Dylan was at a loss for words. "Hello and thanks for calling this, ah... meeting." She swallowed, "Um, everyone thought you were dead."

"Sure, why wouldn't they? But here I am, in the flesh, breathing, walking, and everything."

"But how?"

"I'll get to that a bit later." He wore a grin, but now it broadened. "I asked you here today because I really can't thank you enough. You solved my murder, so to speak, but most importantly, you found out who did it."

Dylan was weary. "Yes, it's true all the evidence points to Vyra. I think I speak for Dillon as well when I tell you that we are completely satisfied with our proof, but..."

"Well, here she is as my proof of life." Iglesia stood tall. "Sure, Germandt is in the wind, but he'll trip up sooner or later. Anyway, Vyra and I..." He briefly stopped to read the concern on Dylan's face.

"Oh, I bet you're wondering what's going to happen to her now." Igelsia moved closer and gently touched Vyra's shoulder. "Actually, that reminds me of a story that I read in a joke book when I was about, maybe, ten or so. Will you allow me... can I tell it to you now?"

Dylan felt a small stall might be in Vyra's favor. "Sure, why not?"

Igelsia continued, "Let's see if I remember it." He looked off into the distance, and then his gaze returned, and his eyes were clear and steady.

"A traveling salesman pulled up to a farmer working near the front of his fields. The salesman introduced himself from his car window and asked if he could stay with the farmer overnight. The farmer came over and they talked for a minute. Upon agreeing to the terms, the salesman got out and fished his one suitcase from the back seat. As he came around the car, he noticed a pig nuzzling the farmer's pant leg. And, he noticed the pig had one wooden leg. 'That pig sure likes you,' the salesman quipped. 'Oh, for sure,' the farmer said, 'and he's the family favorite.' The salesman bent down to pet the pig, 'And why is that?'

Dylan began shuffling in place, and Iglesia picked up on it.

"No, hang in there, it gets good now." He took a deep breath. "The farmer says, 'Once our boy was playing too near the pond out back and fell in. He started thrashing around and yelling. The pig heard the commotion and broke out of his sty. He ran over and jumped in the water, pulled the boy out, and began mouth-to-mouth resuscitation. This pig saved my boys' lives.'"

Dylan chuckled.

Encouraged, Iglesia went on. "'That's one valuable pig,' said the salesman. 'Oh, you don't know the half of it,' said the farmer. 'Another time, I was on my tractor mowing the tall grass. I was cutting diagonally on a small hill when the tractor fell over and pinned me under it. I shouted for help, and once again the pig heard and busted through the small fence around his pen and ran toward me. It must have been the pig's adrenaline surge, but after he dug around me, he was able to pull me out from under. The pig ran back to the house and alerted the wife, and I was saved.'

Igelsia looked for a reaction, and Dylan gave a small smile. He kept the story going. 'Wow,' the salesman said, 'that might be the most valuable pig ever.' The farmer went on, 'Just a few months ago, our farmhouse caught fire one night. The pig saw the fire and once again broke through the fence and rushed into the house. He ran up the stairs and discovered we had all been overcome by the smoke and were unconscious. So, the pig pulled each one of us out of the burning building, performed CPR, and used his snout to touch 9-1-1 on my iPhone.'"

Now Dylan was invested in the story and leaned forward in anticipation.

“The salesman was astounded. ‘Wow. Wow. Wow. That pig wins the most valuable prize hands down. That pig probably also holds the record for most human saves!’ Then the salesman reviewed the whole story again. He asked the farmer, ‘Helping you all…well…is that how your pig lost his leg?’ The farmer smiled. ‘No, it's just a pig this valuable, well, you can't bring yourself to eat all at once.’”

Dylan started to laugh and thought better of it. All she could think of saying was, "Well, that joke took a dark turn."

Iglesia felt Vyra wrestle slightly with her restraints. He gently brushed her hair from her face and looked up at the detective. "You know, I knew she was smart and ambitious, and I knew that combination would end one of us someday, but I never thought it would end quite like this.” He drifted off into his thoughts.

“Well, anyway, thanks again." He motioned to the man to come and wheel Vyra out. He stopped halfway out of the gym and turned back. "Really, I can't begin to say...well...needless to say your favor to me is repaid in full. I've also wired a token of my appreciation to your firm’s bank account." He looked down at the floor. "It makes me sad to think I won't see you both again, so let’s say goodbye, but hopefully, just for now."

He turned and raced to catch up to Vyra and her pusher. Once again, he briefly stopped to say, “Oh, by the way, can you believe that Vyra wanted me to have the gene patch patents? She’s already transferred them into my name. Isn’t that just so sweet of her?” This time, he vanished through the door.

Dylan turned and let out a sigh of relief. *All done. Successfully, I might add.*

Dylan began a leisurely stroll towards the door. Her thoughts were not done with her. *I wonder what the point of that silly story was. I don't think he was alluding to what was going to happen to Vyra...I mean, he's not going to chop her up over time?*

Dylan's next thought was very sobering. *Bad guys have no morals. And unfortunately, like the song says, 'The bad guys win every once in a while.'* She momentarily tried to decide if she should go after Vyra or not. Ultimately, she shrugged her shoulders. *And let's not forget all the lab techs' deaths she orchestrated and what their families went through.*

Dylan was moving again. *I can't help but sense very bad endings for Vyra and Germandt. More importantly, I just don't know if this feels like justice.*

Dylan's mind settled on one final thought. *But for me, the most important thing is that we both survived this little Lake Zurich adventure. And hopefully, we won't run into Mr. Iglesia ever again.*

Time to go tell Dillon all that happened. Suddenly, the feeling was overwhelming, and she quickened her step. She just couldn't wait to see him and share.

Chapter Twenty-One

The Next Case

Mr. Haus, Mr. Barn, Mr. Bank, Ms. School, and Mr. Museum stood in a neat line within the grand lobby of the Syndicate's lab lobby, their expressions a mix of solemnity and gratitude. The detectives, Dylan and Dillon, were taken aback by this unexpected send-off. It was rare, if not unprecedented, for the Syndicate's directors to personally bid farewell to operatives.

After a series of firm handshakes and heartfelt thanks, the pair gathered their suitcases, the weight of their recent experiences still pressing upon them. Mr. Haus, ever the stoic, took the driver's seat to escort them to the train station.

"I must admit," Mr. Haus began, eyes fixed on the road ahead, "I owe you both an apology."

Dylan and Dillon exchanged surprised glances. An apology from Mr. Haus was as rare as a Swiss summer without tourists.

"I understand you've already said goodbyes to Mr. Iglesia," he continued.

Dylan nodded silently, memories of their final conversation with Iglesia flashing through her mind. The fate of Germandt was likely sealed, but Vyra's ultimate destiny remained a lingering question.

"The other directors," Mr. Haus went on, "have decided to show their appreciation by wiring an additional million dollars each to your firm. They were relieved the Syndicate remained intact and grateful it wasn't one of them who triggered the bomb."

Dillon offered a modest smile. "That's very generous. Please extend our thanks."

Mr. Haus glanced at Dillon through the rearview mirror. "Mr. Iglesia insisted on adding another million to your fee. He said it was only fair, considering you nearly lost your life."

Dylan reached out, intertwining her fingers with Dillon's. The gesture spoke volumes of their shared relief and unspoken bond.

At the train station, the clock's hands aligned with the watch on Dillon’s wrist and their scheduled departure. As the train pulled in, final goodbyes were exchanged. Dylan, with a playful grin, gave an exaggerated wave from the window. To her delight, Mr. Haus responded with a brief, yet genuine, wave.

****

"Happy?" Dillon asked, settling into his seat on the flight back to Daytona.

"Ecstatic!" Dylan replied, her head resting against the seatback, eyes closed. "I still can't believe all we saw yesterday."

"You can thank Liberty for arranging everything. I still don't know how she managed it. She booked us an extra day in the Swiss Alps."

Dylan chuckled. "I know. Let's see if I can recall it all."

Dillon unfolded the itinerary. "We took the train from Zurich to Lauterbrunnen. Then, a gondola up towards Mürren."

Dylan's eyes opened wide. "That gondola went straight up! It swayed every time we passed through a tower. I had to focus on the horizon to avoid looking down."

"Then, a smaller cog train into Mürren itself," Dillon continued. "Remember those loud American guys there to base jump?"

"Yes, but I was too captivated by the mountain scenery to be bothered. I've seen mountains in Colorado, but the Alps are something else."

"My favorite part was the gondola up to the Schilthorn," Dillon said, eyes gleaming.

"Where they filmed part of that James Bond movie," Dylan added.

"Exactly. They played the theme song as we exited the gondola. The dazzling views of the Jungfrau and the Eiger were breathtaking."

"After lunch, we traveled back down to Lauterbrunnen and took a helicopter to Zermatt," Dylan recalled. "We were lucky to have a clear view of the Matterhorn. Everyone says it's usually hidden in clouds."

"It was awe-inspiring," Dillon agreed. "Second only to the street vendor bratwurst I had."

"Stop it!" Dylan laughed. "That brought us to this flight back from Geneva. It was insane to fit all that into one day. I need to return when we have more time."

"Well, we made six million dollars from this case. That should buy us a week or two next time."

As the plane began its taxi, both detectives said in unison, "Time to go home."

****

Upon landing in Daytona Beach, the pair switched off airplane mode on their phones. Screens lit up with a barrage of emails, calls, and texts. They used the taxi time to sift through the messages.

Dillon listened to his last voicemail. "Oh, oh!"

"What is it?" Dylan asked, sensing urgency.

"Remember our starry night train murder case and the cartel leader involved?"

Dylan nodded, recalling the intense ordeal.

"Well, it's his voice on this message. I'm sure of it!"

"What did he say?"

Dillon put his phone on speaker and played the message. The voice was low and whispery. "You know who this is... I'm in big trouble... I need you both down here in Puerto Vallarta today... Someone is trying to kill me!"

Dylan's eyes widened. "Puerto Vallarta? That's Cartel territory. It's risky."

Dillon nodded. "But if he's reaching out, he must be desperate."

Dylan sighed. "Looks like our next case just found us."

That afternoon, Dylan and Dillon convened in their office, the voicemail still fresh in their minds.

Dylan began. "I was right. Puerto Vallarta is a known hotspot for Cartel activity."

Dillon nodded. "We need to be cautious. I know you don't want to hear this, but if our old contact is in danger, it might be in our best interest to help him."

Dylan leaned back. "This won't be easy. But with our experience, we can navigate it. And I think I have another idea that might help us."

Dillon smiled. "Then let's prepare. Puerto Vallarta awaits."

www.ingramcontent.com/pod-product-compliance
Lightning Source LLC
LaVergne TN
LVHW022104200926
848481LV00003B/1058
* 9 7 9 8 8 6 9 3 2 9 6 1 5 *